How to
Make Money
using Etsy

How to

Make Money

using Etsy

A *Guide* to the
Online Marketplace
for *Crafts* and
Handmade Products

Timothy Adam

WILEY

John Wiley & Sons, Inc.

Published by John Wiley & Sons, Inc., Hoboken, New Jersey.
Published simultaneously in Canada.

For general information on our other products and services or for technical support, please contact our Customer Care Department within the United States at (800) 762-2974, outside the United States at (317) 572-3993 or fax (317) 572-4002.

Wiley also publishes its books in a variety of electronic formats. Some content that appears in print may not be available in electronic books. For more information about Wiley products, visit our web site at www.wiley.com.

Library of Congress Cataloging-in-Publication Data:

978-0-470-94456-1 (paper)
978-1-118-03382-1 (ebk)
978-1-118-03383-8 (ebk)
978-1-118-03384-5 (ebk)

Printed in the United States of America
10 9 8 7 6 5 4 3 2

I want to thank my wife Christina for the constant encouragement that she gives me to push forward and keep designing, creating, helping, and writing. I also want to thank the handmade community for reading and visiting my blogs and for your support over the years. The real star of the show is my little boy Camden Reid: born July 31, 2010 during the writing process of this book. Thanks buddy, for being such a calm and happy baby.

Contents

Preface

While searching for a direction for my metal furniture and art, I stumbled upon Etsy. Etsy quickly became my new home and launching pad for many adventures. New designs, connections with artists, learning, blogging, and teaching can all be traced back to the day I joined Etsy. *How to Make Money Using Etsy* came about because of a need that I saw in the crafting and handmade scene for a guide to selling arts and crafts online. Packed full of information, starting with setting up your Etsy shop, to interviews with top sellers and bloggers, this guide is designed with all levels of sellers in mind.

Introduction

Art and design have not always been a part of my life. Growing up in Northeast Ohio, creating and designing were the furthest things from my mind. I played soccer all my life and was always interested in science. I studied environmental engineering in college and wanted to become a park ranger. Shortly after finishing college in Ohio, I moved to Grand Rapids, Michigan, to get my degree in secondary education, and be near Christina, the girl I was going to marry. In the summer of 2004, Christina's sister, who is a furniture designer, needed some help with a few metal projects. I wanted to lend a hand in building these projects but, at the time, had never even welded two pieces of scrap metal together. I wound up taking a welding course and fell in love with the trade. I mean, who wouldn't love melting metal? The summer of 2004 changed my life, and it was then that I realized what I wanted to do for the rest of my life. I found my passion and my creative outlet that I didn't even realize I needed.

Taking the skills and tools from that summer experience, I went back to Grand Rapids, where I started creating and designing furniture. I designed and built a portfolio of about 20 pieces and I hit the road running. Grand Rapids, Michigan, and its surrounding communities are packed full of galleries and shops, but with such an industrial-modern furniture style, it was difficult to find shops that would carry my work. Most shops did not have the room to carry furniture, until one day I walked into a shop in East Grand Rapids. I remember sitting down with the shop owner and her business partner as they looked through my portfolio. I was so used to being rejected, I was surprised and overwhelmed when they started pointing out pieces they wanted in their shop. This was the turning point. This was when I knew that I could do what I love—and love what I do!

Galleries, shops, custom work, and art shows drove my part-time metal design business for about three years. This was all on top of my regular full-time job, so it kept me very busy, but I loved every minute of it, so I wasn't about to stop. If you've ever been in an art or craft show, you know how time consuming they are! Art and craft shows are an amazing way to get your name out locally, but they can be very time consuming and sometimes not even profitable. It was in 2005, in the middle of the art and craft show "season" of my life that Christina and I got married, and another new chapter of my life began.

For the next two years, I pressed on with the art shows, approaching galleries to try to get my work accepted, and I had a handful of custom jobs for clients here and there. I loved these three methods of exposure, but I kept wishing there was a way I could get my work visible to more people in more places than just West Michigan.

In January 2007, one of my good friends told me about Etsy. She talked about how you could list an item for four months for only 20 cents! The thought of only spending 20 cents to have my metal furniture online for the whole world to see was enough for me to investigate further into the world of Etsy. After reading success stories and learning more about how to set up an Etsy shop, I jumped in headfirst—that's pretty much how I am about everything I get involved in.

At the time of launching my Etsy shop, I had no prior knowledge of the Internet besides checking e-mail, shopping on eBay, and watching funny videos. I knew my wife had something called a Facebook page, but I had no clue what it was and I wasn't really interested in finding out. I had no personal experience with product photography, search engine optimization (SEO), online marketing, or even selling anything online. Luckily, Christina and I are good friends with an amazing photographer, and he helped me shoot some of my furniture pieces so I could start listing them on Etsy.

With my drive and passion to get my furniture out there, I filled my Etsy shop with metal. Three weeks after opening my Etsy shop, I made my first sale! It was a $20 candle holder that I had sold many of at art shows. I still remember that feeling of knowing someone in another state found my candle holder in my Etsy shop, liked it, and purchased it! This was just the beginning of amazing things to come. Etsy had given me a way to get my metal in front of people that would never have known about little old me. I had finally expanded my reach from West Michigan to the rest of the world.

During the first few weeks of selling on Etsy, I discovered the Etsy forums and community, an ever-growing, ever-changing resource of knowledge. I was chatting in the forums one evening when a seller mentioned that they liked my metal furniture, home accessories, and art, but I needed to expand my shop into the jewelry scene. Being a welder metal guy, I thought jewelry was not for me at all. But after browsing Etsy a bit and seeing other amazing metal jewelry artists, I decided to try my hand at jewelry.

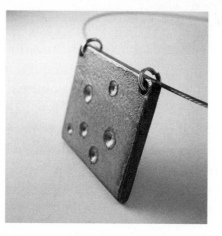

By creating jewelry, I found a way to express my creativity in a smaller, less time-consuming way than I did with my furniture. I love expressing my artistic ability and style in a one-inch-by-one-inch piece of scrap metal. The incorporation of jewelry and smaller, less expensive items into my Etsy shop was the change I needed to start selling more items and eventually quit my day job.

Through hard work and dedication, I taught myself what I needed to know to maintain a successful Etsy business. Since first joining Etsy in 2007, I have continually strived to improve my photography skills, customer service, and online marketing, and keep designing new lines of product. *How to Make Money Using Etsy* is designed to teach you what you need to know to successfully set up an Etsy shop and take the fear out of selling your handmade goods online. You will also learn the important skills to promote your Etsy shop on Facebook, Twitter, and your very own blog.

All About Etsy

Etsy's mission is to enable everyone to make a living, making the things they love, and to connect makers with buyers from around the world. Founded in 2005, Etsy is a worldwide handmade community that spans over 150 countries. To me, as a seller, Etsy is a life changer, and as a buyer, I know when I make an Etsy purchase, I'm helping artists like myself.

Is Etsy the right online marketplace for you? Take a look at what some Etsy sellers and buyers are saying about Etsy and decide for yourself.

Etsy has given me courage as a seller to try new things! It was a new way for me to be able to do what I love. Easy to get started and maintain a shop. My creativity has come alive! As a buyer, I love it because I can make personal contact with those who actually MAKE what I purchase. That connection is very gratifying to me as a customer.

Etsy is an ENABLER!! They enabled me to be a successful at-home Mom!

I love Etsy! First thing I love is the simplicity of the design. I dislike clutter of ads all over, so Etsy does this well. I found all the things one needs to do to set up a shop super easy, and signed up for the weekly e-mails on what is new. I stay abreast in the forums, the Storque (Etsy's blog). I do tons of treasuries. That is where we get to pick twelve products from Etsy artists. One can even be our own now. Then it goes public for all to see. Just a fun thing, but it gets more views for those who see them. I also tweet my treasury to help out the artists I pick. I also created my own team, after finding out how many people right here in my own town were on Etsy. We call ourselves OCEAN—Oregon Coast Etsy Artist Network. This has helped me grow and share what we learn. All of us are older women who want to make a living, selling our art online. I love the new "Rearrange Your Shop" for our shop as this is just like a treasury now. I can do color and themes each month. I find the fees fair. I have no complaints with Etsy at all. I joined over a 1/2 year ago. I started with really poor photos, and did not know anything. I am doing 100 percent better now, and think I am going to go full time with it now. Because of Etsy, a retail shop in Las Vegas saw me, and I now sell wholesale to them! Life is good on Etsy!

Overall, Etsy is amazing for the small-time home crafter or small business owner. My partner and I launched our business on Etsy after deciding that we would be work-at-home parents and not get a "real" job. Etsy has given us so many opportunities in such a short period of time. We have a ton of support from:

1. *Fellow sellers picking us to be in "treasuries," some of which make it to the front page of Etsy (great for exposure!)*

2. *Admin picking us to be featured in e-mails*

3. *"Storque" (Etsy's blog) articles, which have taught us 60 percent of everything we now know about marketing and selling*

4. *Etsy forums, which has been great for asking questions, getting answers, and searching the*

archives for past discussions (even on topics unrelated to Etsy)

5. *E-mail blasts, which include great finds for the buyer as well as seller's tips and tricks*

The Etsy administration does a great job at addressing concerns, responding to e-mails, and in general, just continuing to upgrade Etsy to make it an intuitive, user-friendly experience for both seller and buyer.

As a buyer, Etsy is perfect for finding something hand-made and one off so I won't see anyone else walking down the street wearing the same thing as me. As a seller, it's a unique place to sell around the world even when I'm asleep! Love it.

Etsy Defined—Etsy Terms You Should Know

Alchemy: Here is where buyers can request custom work.

Avatar: Your avatar is a small icon that shows up by your shop name throughout Etsy. The most prominent place is in one's Etsy shop. You will also see your avatar in the Etsy forums and various other places when you leave a comment.

B&M: Brick-and-mortar store. A physical store, like a gallery or boutique.

Convo (conversation): A conversation, or more commonly referred to in the Etsy community as "Convo," is Etsy's internal e-mail system. Every user can be contacted through the Convo system.

Etsians: Everyone in the Etsy community, sellers and buyers.

Newbie: A newbie is a seller or buyer that is new to Etsy. There is no set length of time you have to be on Etsy to not be considered a newbie.

Feedback: Feedback is the rating system that Etsy has in place for sellers and buyers. Once an item is purchased, positive, neutral, and negative feedback can be given.

Forum: The Etsy Forum is where sellers and buyers can go to connect and learn from the community. Promote your shop and get real business advice. The Etsy Forum is closely moderated by the Etsy admin.

Hearts (favorites): Hearts are a user's way to mark an item or an entire Etsy shop as your favorite. You can view these hearted items and shops in "Your Etsy" area.

Kiss and Make Up: When you receive negative or neutral feedback from a seller or a buyer, you have the ability to have them reverse or change it. Through the "Kiss and Make Up" system, both parties have to agree, and it can be changed.

Marking: Word used in the Etsy Forum to mark a forum post so one can go back and find it later.

Public Profile: Your public profile is where you can tell a little about yourself. Both sellers and buyers have a public profile.

SEO: Search engine optimization. Getting your shop and items found on Google.

Shop Local: Find out what shops are in your area.

Shop Policies: Buyers want to find out if they can return an item, or how long it may take to have their item shipped. Your shop policies are the place to explain in detail important information about your shop.

Storque: The Storque is Etsy's blog. You will find tips for selling and amazing Etsy finds.

Teams: An Etsy Team is a group of sellers gathered to help one another. There are teams for jewelry sellers, painters, knitters, states, cities, etc. You name it, and there is probably a team for it!

Treasury: The Etsy Treasury is a user-curated shopping gallery. You can create lists of your favorite items for the world to see.

Virtual Labs: Live classes, chats, and a ton of resources for the Etsy community.

Your Etsy: ''Your Etsy'' is a user's admin area. This is where items are managed and your shop setup is located.

The Etsy Community

The Etsy community plays a huge role in the success of sellers and spreading the word about Etsy and the handmade movement. The Etsy community is made up of three very important parts.

The first part is the Etsy Storque, which is Etsy's blog. You will find the latest Etsy news, handmade trends, success stories, and even Etsy's Seller Handbook. The Seller Handbook is packed full of answers to any questions you may have about selling on Etsy. Along with Etsy's blog comes the Success Newsletters. These newsletters are very well put together and are designed to help sellers improve their shops on a weekly basis. I strongly suggest you sign up right away so you can start receiving the newsletter in your inbox.

Second are the Etsy Teams. The Etsy Teams are groups of like-minded sellers that are there to help one another. Team members are there to answer questions and help promote each other. Etsy even gives out Team grants to help with promotion and advertising.

The third vital part to the Etsy community is the Etsy Forum. The Etsy Forum is a vibrant, live forum, filled with sellers and buyers. If you have a question about selling on Etsy, or running a small business in general, the Etsy community is ready to supply the answers. You will find an admin announcement section that will keep you up to date with all the latest Etsy updates. There is a site help section for when you are wondering how something works. The business section is set up for business topics and is a tremendous resource full of information from other sellers and the

Etsy admin. The critique section is where you would head if you are looking to have your shop or items critiqued by other sellers. It is always good to get a second, third, or even hundredth opinion. The promotion section is a fast-paced, never stagnant forum. You can shamelessly promote your shop and items here. There are even more sections to the Etsy Forum . . . it is definitely a place you should visit to learn and promote.

There are more parts to the Etsy community on and off Etsy. With the Etsy community in place, Etsy will continue to grow along with its sellers.

2

Getting to Know You and Your Product

Before you start this process, let's do a quick brainstorming session to get a better understanding of your product. You know your handmade product best, and you know what you know. Do you know what you need to improve on? Survey yourself using the following questions, and write these answers down to help you narrow down what you want to sell, what you need to learn, and what you are the best at!

Basic Product Questions

- What do I make? (List it all)

- Do I love what I make?

- What do I want my main product focus to be?

- What sets my product apart from the competition?

- What technique do I do better than the competition?

- What is the price range of my product?

- Is it easy to ship?

- What is my target market? (Who will be interested in my product?)

- What are 10 possible words that describe my craft?

- Do I have a "good" digital camera?

Marketing and Branding

- Do I have a blog?

- Do I have a Twitter account?

- Do I have a Facebook account (personal profile and fan page)?

- Do I know how to effectively use the above social media tools to promote my products?

- Do I understand search engine optimization (SEO) and how it helps with traffic from search engines?

- What keywords or phrases fit my products, and do I know how to properly place them?

- Do I know how to design a banner, or know someone who can do it for me?

- Do I know how to take product pictures that sell my products?

- Do I have business cards?

General Online Selling

- How many hours per week can I dedicate to selling my product?

- How will buyers find my items?

- Do I have a PayPal account?

- What shipping should I use—United States Postal Service, FedEx, or UPS?

- Do I need to collect sales tax, and how do I do that?

Product Research

When getting ready to sell your handmade goods online, it is important to know what is selling, trending, and what is hot. There are a few sites that can tell you what is being searched on Google and other search engines. With that information, we can determine what is being bought online. These tests, tools, and searches will help you determine the direction you want to take your products. These tests are not 100 percent foolproof ways of determining how items will sell, but they will give you an idea how the market is for your handmade goods. This is a great opportunity to really get to know your products and what people are searching for out there on the Internet.

Basic Google Search

The very first simple search you can do right off the bat is on Google. Go to google.com and type your product category in the Google search box. For this case, I am going to use "crochet" as the

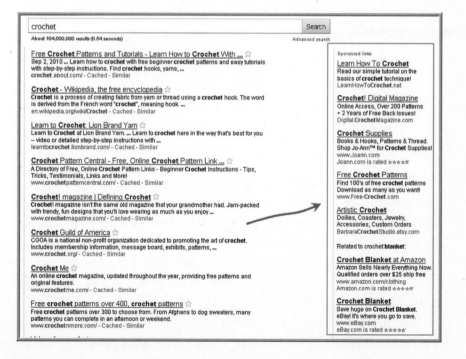

example. When you type this in, hit the search button, and see advertisers on the right-hand side, you know it is a good niche to sell in. A niche is a small category within a larger one. For example, "crochet" is a smaller niche within handmade products, and "crocheted hats" is even smaller yet. Getting very specific will help narrow things down and really tell us important information about your handmade products.

Google Trends

The first tool we are going to look at to help us determine if your handmade products are going to sell is Google Trends. Google Trends lets you **compare the world's interest** in your chosen niche markets over an extended period of time. For example, I entered *crochet, knitting,* and *yarn* and discovered some significant spikes in the interest in all three in the past 12 months (shown in the following graphic).

You may enter up to five terms and see how often they've been searched for on Google over time. You can look at past years or the

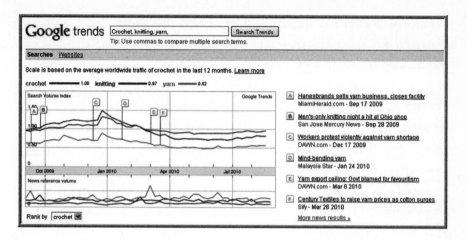

past 30 days. It also displays how frequently your terms have appeared in Google News stories, and which geographic regions have searched for them most often.

Google Insights

The next site is also more of a general overview of the searches for the niche you are looking to sell in. Google Insights give you a look at the search trends over a long period of time.

In the following example, I searched the same three words—*crochet, knitting, yarn*—and you can see the trend in searches from 2008 to 2010.

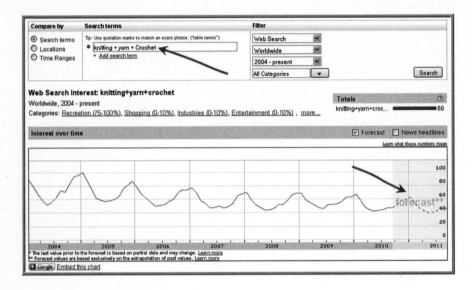

Google Insights also give you one more advantage. It gives you some of the top searches according to the terms you entered. You can see below the top searches and the rising searches.

Search terms				
Top searches		**Rising searches**	
1. knitting patterns	100	1. yarn harlot	+350%
2. crochet patterns	75	2. tejidos a crochet	+250%
3. knitting pattern	65	3. knitting help	+200%
4. crochet pattern	50	4. tejido crochet	+90%
5. knit	50	5. crochet flower	+80%
6. knitting patterns free	40	6. loom knitting	+80%
7. free crochet patterns	35	7. crochet baby blanket	+70%
8. how to crochet	30	8. double crochet	+50%
9. knitting yarn	30	9. crochet hook	+40%
10. knitting factory	25	10. knitting for beginners	+40%
Google Embed this table		Google Embed this table	

Google Insights also provides you with a look at the location of these searches. You can see what country is searching for your product the most.

Regional interest		⑦ Region City
1. United States	————— 100	
2. Bangladesh	———— 75	
3. Canada	———— 66	
4. Australia	——— 57	
5. New Zealand	——— 55	
6. United Kingdom	——— 46	
7. Pakistan	—— 40	
8. Cuba	—— 38	
9. Chile	—— 37	
10. South Africa	—— 36	

Search volume index
0 ▮▮▮▮▮▮▮ 100
⊞ View change over time ⑦

Google Trends and Google Insights are both great indicators to know if your niche is being searched, but there is much more to this process.

The next step in the product research process is to search and see if there are popular magazines selling in your niche. Popular magazines can tell us if people are reading about your products, and if they find them interesting. The first site I like to visit is Magazines.com. First, you want to look at the top categories they have on the left-hand side. These are the top magazine categories that are selling right now. If your craft/art/products fall into these categories, that's a good sign.

Click on the "More Categories" button and find the hobbies section. You will see the arts and crafts section right at the top. Check out the top-selling magazines in the arts and crafts sections.

Now let's take it a bit further and search our crochet niche and see the results. In the following picture, there are a number of knitting magazines. This is a good thing when you see magazines that are selling in your niche. If you are not seeing any results for your products, that is OK. At this point, you are just getting a feel for the market. Not seeing any magazines does not mean you shouldn't sell what you make on Etsy.

eBay Pulse

eBay Pulse is a daily snapshot of what the current search and item trends are on eBay. You can find info on popular searches, largest stores and most-watched items.

Although the eBay Pulse page shows an overview of the entire eBay marketplace, you can use the drop-down menu to refine and filter the lists to show content for specific categories on eBay. Check out the following picture; you can see the trend for crafts on eBay. You can also see the largest stores selling craft-related items.

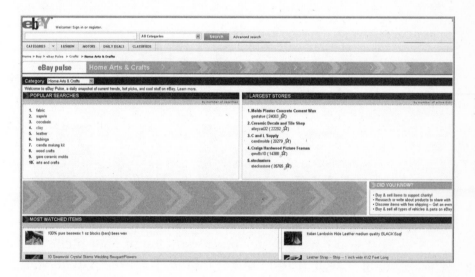

Etsy Search

Now it's time to check out the competition over on Etsy. There are a few easy ways to find out who, if anyone, is selling what you make.

The first way to find out if anyone is selling what you make is to do a simple Etsy search. Type your subject in the search box at the top of Etsy's site and hit "Search." Use quotations around the word or phrase to get more of a focused search result. While you are looking around, stop by some of the Etsy shops and see what types of items these shops are selling, and ask yourself a few questions:

- Are the prices close to what I was going to sell my items for?

- How will my pictures compare?

- How will my shipping prices compare?

- How will my shop policies compare?

Now that you have a better understanding of your niche and what is being searched and bought online, you are ready to start setting up your Etsy shop.

3

Your Etsy Shop Setup

The first step to setting up your Etsy shop is picking a username. Your Etsy username is going to be the name of your Etsy shop, so you need to pick this carefully. This is the first place in your Etsy shop where you will start the SEO process. You will also need to find out if the dot-com is available and if there are any other businesses out there with the same name you want to use.

SEO Defined

Wikipedia states that "**search engine optimization (SEO) is the process of improving the visibility of a web site or a web page in search engines** via the 'natural' or unpaid ('organic' or 'algorithmic') search results."

SEO will play a huge role in getting your handmade goods from your Etsy shop found on Google and other search engines. For your Etsy shop, we are going to focus on finding and properly placing strong keywords. Your Etsy shop name is important for SEO of your shop, because your shop name will be included in the URL address of your shop, and this is the first place Google looks for keywords.

http://www.etsy.com/shop/TimothyAdamDesigns

Since your Etsy shop name is so important, you need to put some thought and research into it. The best research tool for

17

searching for strong keywords is the Google Adwords Key Word Tool. I will be referring back to this process several times so make sure you learn it well.

Keyword Research

The quickest way to find the Google keyword tool is to go to Google and search "Google Keyword Tool." The first option will be what you we are looking for. When you first visit the page, you will be asked to enter a few letters to determine if you are a real person. This is just a security measure.

To get started, just enter the general category of your hand-made product. I am going to stick with the crochet theme.

Once you hit the search button, you will see suggested keywords and phrases in the left column. In the middle column you will see the competition for ad space in the Google search and you will notice the Global monthly searches. These are the three columns we are going to focus on.

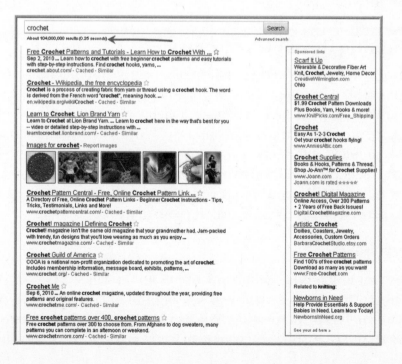

At first glance, we can see that we are going to want to use the word *crochet* in the name of our Etsy shop. This word is searched millions of times per month on Google. Just because a keyword is searched millions or even thousands of times per month does not necessarily make it a strong keyword. We have to look at the competition or competing pages. Let's take a look at the keyword *crochet* again on Google.

Just as before, you are going to see there are advertisers on the right-hand side of the Google search. This is good thing! Take a look right under the search box, and you will see how many pages Google is showing for the keyword *crochet:* 104 million. Even with the keyword *crochet* being searched 2 million times per month, the fact that the competing page number is so high means it is going to be tough for this keyword to be found on Google. We also want to look at what type of web sites is near the top of the search. In this case, we are looking at some strong sites, such as About.com, CrochetMagazine.com, Crochet.org, and Crochetme.com. With these strong web sites sitting at the top of the Google search, ranking in a good spot on Google for the keyword *crochet* will be impossible. All hope is not lost, because it is now time to get creative and find some strong keywords that could possibly fit as an Etsy shop name.

We know we want to use the keyword *crochet* because that is our main category that we are going to sell in on Etsy. Think of some words and phrases that would fit with your category. Your shop name is important because it will be with you and your business for a long time.

Walking through Your Etsy

Once you have picked your Etsy username/shop name, you are ready to start putting your shop together. To find the admin area of your Etsy shop, make sure you are logged in and look for the blue link at the top that says "Your Etsy." Your Etsy admin area is packed full of information and ways to get your shop ready to go. In this section, I will walk you through each section and give you tips that will help you set up your Etsy shop, list your first items, and get you on your way to making your first sale.

Purchases

The first link on the right-hand side that you will see is your purchases. This is where you will see all of the items you have purchased or will be purchasing. You can sort your purchased items by month and year, and see if your item has been shipped or not. There

Your Account
- Purchases
- Feedback
- Favorites
- Public Profile
- Account
- Your Bill
- Alchemy
- Applications

Your Shop
- Items
  - Add New Item
  - Currently for Sale
  - Inactive Listings
  - Expired Listings
  - Featured Listings
  - Shipping
- Orders
  - Sold Orders
  - Cancel an Order
  - Sales Stats
- Shop Settings
  - Info & Appearance

Important! If you collect sales tax, please set tax rates for the new Checkout.

Currently for Sale (52) View your public shop.

Can't find a listing you were editing? View inactive listings.

[ ] Renew ? Deactivate ? Delete

Title	In Stock	Price	▼ Listed	Expires	Featured	
Japanese cherry tree	1	$83.00 USD	Oct. 28, 2010	Feb. 28, 2011	★	Edit Promote
Steel Earring Tree - Earring Display Rack	1	$42.00 USD	Oct. 27, 2010	Feb. 27, 2011	★	Edit Promote
Simple Necklace Tree - T Bar Display	1	$38.40 USD	Oct. 27, 2010	Feb. 27, 2011	★	Edit Promote
Tiny Twig Earring Tree Jewelry Rack	1	$18.00 USD	Oct. 22, 2010	Feb. 22, 2011	★	Edit Promote
On Sale Small Earring Tree	1	$27.00 USD	Oct. 22, 2010	Feb. 22, 2011	★	Edit Promote
flat round beads	1	$19.00 USD	Oct. 21, 2010	Feb. 21, 2011	★	Edit Promote
On Sale Very Tiny	1	$6.40 USD	Oct. 20, 2010	Feb. 20, 2011	★	Edit

are links directly to the seller and the invoice of your purchase, so you can view all the details. Etsy also makes it easy to report an item that has not been shipped. In the right-hand top corner you will find a link "Report a purchase you never received." If you have not received an item that you purchased, this form is simple to fill out.

Your Account
- Purchases
- Feedback
- Favorites
- Public Profile
- Account
- Your Bill
- Alchemy
- Applications

Your Shop
- Items
  - Add New Item
  - Currently for Sale
  - Inactive Listings
  - Expired Listings
  - Featured Listings
  - Shipping
- Orders
  - Sold Orders
  - Cancel an Order
  - Sales Stats
- Shop Settings
  - Info & Appearance
  - Shipping & Payment
  - Options
- Promote
  - Referrals

Important! If you collect sales tax, please set tax rates for the new Checkout.

Currently for Sale (51) View your public shop.

Can't find a listing you were editing? View inactive listings.

[ ] Renew ? Deactivate ? Delete

Title	In Stock	Price	▼ Listed	Expires	Featured	
Japanese cherry tree	1	$83.00 USD	Nov. 2, 2010	Mar. 2, 2011	★	Edit Promote
vintage camera	1	$37.00 USD	Oct. 31, 2010	Mar. 28, 2011	★	Edit Promote
523 series cut rectangle	1	$38.00 USD	Oct. 31, 2010	Mar. 28, 2011	★	Edit Promote
Japanese cherry tree	1	$83.00 USD	Oct. 28, 2010	Feb. 28, 2011	★	Edit Promote
Steel Earring Tree - Earring Display Rack	1	$42.00 USD	Oct. 27, 2010	Feb. 27, 2011	★	Edit Promote
Simple Necklace Tree - T Bar Display	1	$38.40 USD	Oct. 27, 2010	Feb. 27, 2011	★	Edit Promote
Tiny Twig Earring Tree Jewelry Rack	1	$18.00 USD	Oct. 22, 2010	Feb. 22, 2011	★	Edit Promote
On Sale Small Earring Tree	1	$27.00 USD	Oct. 22, 2010	Feb. 22, 2011	★	Edit Promote

Feedback

Feedback is a vital part of an Etsy seller's business. Just like other sites, buyers will look at a seller's feedback before purchasing an item. Feedback can come from two places. If you buy an item, a seller will leave

> **Tip**
> Buying items when you first start up your Etsy shop is a quick way to gain feedback without making a sale.

you feedback, and this counts toward your total shop feedback. The second way you will get feedback is when buyers buy from you. Once an item is purchased from your shop, the buyer has the opportunity to leave feedback.

As a seller, you want to do everything you can to keep your feedback positive. Good customer service practices will help you keep your feedback positive. Filling out your shop policies and letting your buyers know exactly what your shop is about will also help. For example, if your buyers know about your return policy before they buy, then they won't be surprised later if they need to return something.

In the feedback section you will notice three tabs. The first tab is your completed feedback. This is the feedback that both buyers and sellers left for you. You can see all the feedback for every transaction right here. You can sort your feedback by buyers, sellers, and feedback you left for others.

The second tab across the top is feedback that is waiting to be sent. These can be from items that were bought from your shop or items that you have bought from other Etsy sellers. This is your opportunity to say something nice about a transaction that went smoothly or something negative about a transaction that went south. You can view the invoice, write a sentence or two, and even add an appreciation photo. My customers often hang their jewelry on jewelry trees they bought from my shop and then take pictures of it. I love seeing how others' jewelry looks hanging on my trees!

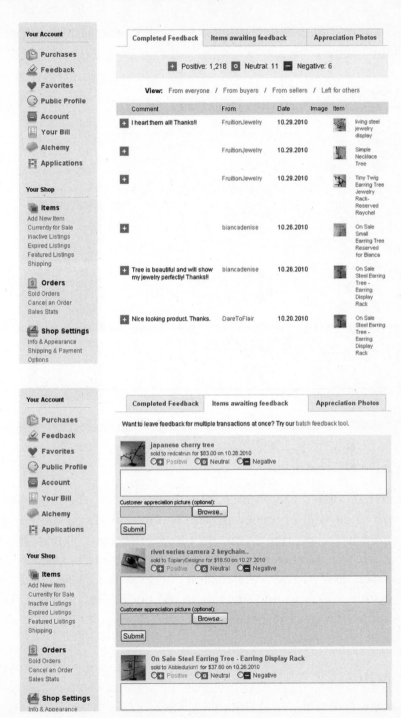

The third tab is where you can view all your customer appreciation pictures.

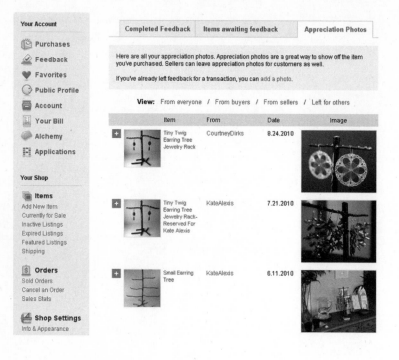

Negative Feedback

Negative feedback can happen. The more you sell, the more likely you are to encounter someone who is unhappy. Even though the customer is always right, you can't make everyone happy. If you do receive negative or even neutral feedback, there is a way to get it reversed. Etsy provides sellers and buyers with a "Kiss and Make Up" option. You can find this link in red under the feedback. This is a simple process, but both parties have to agree before the feedback can be changed.

Favorites

Browsing Etsy is fun and addicting. There are millions of items to look through, so Etsy makes it simple for you to remember what

Your Account

- Purchases
- Feedback
- Favorites
- Public Profile
- Account
- Your Bill
- Alchemy
- Applications

Your Shop

- Items
  Add New Item
  Currently for Sale
  Inactive Listings
  Expired Listings
  Featured Listings
  Shipping

- Orders
  Sold Orders
  Cancel an Order
  Sales Stats

Kiss & Make Up

Item: Simple Necklace Tree - Reserved For Donna
$25.00
transaction # 29396965

Buyer: Feedback: 377, 100% pos.
Location:

Original Feedback: You received neutral feedback on
Didn't anticipate such a rustic appearance; but still nice for my needs.

Status:

You are initiating the kiss and make up right now. Once you click the submit button below, Hithyldy will have to agree to it and leave new feedback. Then the agreement will be made public.

Do you want to kiss & make up?
- Yes
- No

Leave new feedback here:
Positive

[text box]

Submit

shops and items are your favorites. This section is where you will find all your favorite items and shops.

Adding an item or shop to your favorites is simple. When you are browsing through Etsy, look for the "Favorite" button. Based

Your Account

- Purchases
- Feedback
- Favorites
- Public Profile
- Account
- Your Bill
- Alchemy
- Applications

Your Shop

- Items
  Add New Item
  Currently for Sale
  Inactive Listings
  Expired Listings
  Featured Listings
  Shipping

- Orders
  Sold Orders
  Cancel an Order
  Sales Stats

- Shop Settings
  Info & Appearance
  Shipping & Payment

Favorite Items	Favorite Shops	Suggested Shops

Share

Large Brass Owl necklace
by unexpectedexpectancy
Sold

DREAM Travel Candle - Lavender, Bergamot, Sandalwood
by MysticBliss
$2.99 USD

Challenge from my Friends Quilt
by mageez
$177.00 USD

Camera Handmade Lampwork Bead
by maybeads
$9.00 USD

Art Tile Blue Roses -- Ceramic ArtTiles for Mosaics, Jewelry, Magnets and more
by ArtTileMosaics
Sold

A Love Story - Fine Art Photography- 8 x 10 Matted Photograph 11 x 14
by CrescentCreations
Sold

Tweet Christmas Tree Decoration White and Gold Snow Bird
by feltmeupdesigns
Sold

Rectangular Box Pendant with Floral Patterned Brass
by DownToTheWireDesigns
Sold

Lovely Fiona the Owl Leather Keychain (Red)
by leatherprince
Sold

coaster squares - vintage green
by yorktownroad
Sold

Vintage Metal Working School Film Slide Picture Projector
by TheLovelys
Sold

Black Bird on Tree Branch Cup and Saucer
by baileydoesntbark
Sold

on the items that you have picked as your favorites, the suggested items tab will show you items you may like. You can fine-tune your suggested items by clicking the "X" on an item that doesn't fit and the suggested shop tool will get smarter.

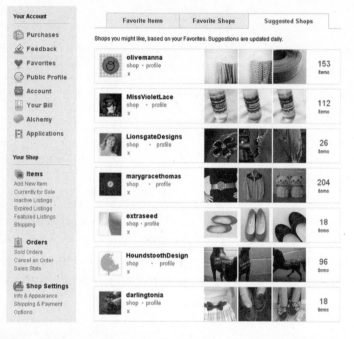

Here's where you'll find where you'll "heart" or "favorite" an item.

Public Profile

Your public profile is important for connecting with your buyers. In this section, you can add your avatar and location, write a profile, and more.

Your avatar is seen on the main page of your shop and throughout the Etsy community. Your avatar can be a picture of you, your products, or anything you want it to be. Etsy also allows you to connect your avatar with Facebook. This makes your Etsy avatar the same as your Facebook profile picture. When you change your Facebook profile picture, your Etsy avatar will change automatically.

Next is your location. Adding your location is simple, but it's also very important because buyers are interested in where you are located. Your location shows up on the main page of your shop for buyers to see.

Writing your profile is next. Tell your buyers about yourself. Don't be afraid to get a little personal here. A lot of people like to learn about the artists they're buying from, so feel free to add details about your life, your family, your hobbies, or anything that may be of interest to your potential clients. I also like to add a link to my shop policies.

Account

Your account information is next on the list. Here is where you will find your password, e-mail address, billing info, privacy settings, and more.

The first tab is your account information. Here, you can change your e-mail address and password.

The second tab is your preferences for your shop. You can pick what information shows up when you click the "Your Etsy"

Account | Preferences | Privacy | Shipping Addresses | Billing

Preferences

Your Etsy Shortcut

Choose where you'd like the "Your Etsy" link in the header to take you.

Currently For Sale ▾
Currently For Sale
Orders (Sold)
Your Purchases

Treasury Mature Content Filtering

Learn more about content filtering.

⦿ **Filter mature content** from Treasury results
◯ **Show me everything** in Treasury results, including mature content

Currency

Select the currency you would like to see prices in.

$	United States Dollar USD	Kč	Czech Koruna CZK	₱	Philippine Peso PHP
$	Canadian Dollar CAD	kr	Danish Krone DKK	$	Singapore Dollar SOD
€	Euro EUR	$	Hong Kong Dollar HKD	kr	Swedish Krona SEK
£	British Pound GBP	Ft	Hungarian Forint HUF	CHF	Swiss Franc CHF
$	Australian Dollar AUD	₪	Israeli Shekel ILS	฿	Thai Baht THB
¥	Japanese Yen JPY	RM	Malaysian Ringgit MYR	NT$	Taiwan New Dollar TWD
		$	Mexican Peso MXN	zł	Polish Zloty PLN
		$	New Zealand Dollar NZD	R$	Brazilian Real BRL
		kr	Norwegian Krone NOK		

button. You can set your mature content filter and choose the currency you would like to see prices in. Etsy currently provides 23 currencies to pick from. Under the third tab, you will find your privacy settings. Set your favorites and purchases either private or public.

Account | Preferences | Privacy | Shipping Addresses | Billing

Privacy

Favorites

Who can see your favorites?

⦿ **Everyone** (public)
◯ **Only you** (private)

Purchases

Who can see your purchases?

⦿ **Everyone** (public)
◯ **Only you** (private, between you and the shop owner)

Update Privacy Settings

The fourth tab is where you can add a shipping address. The fifth tab is where you will find your credit card information.

Your Bill

This is the location of your Etsy bill. You will be billed by Etsy for two things. First is listing items. For every item you list in your Etsy shop, you will be charged 20 cents. Etsy also charges 3.5 percent of every sale. The easiest way to pay your Etsy bill is to pay with PayPal, although you can also use your credit card.

Your Etsy Bill   Read how billing works

Due by Oct 15:
$0.00
Total unpaid fees minus the current month.

Total balance:
$13.54 USD
This is the total of all your unpaid fees.

You have no overdue fees.

Manual payment
MAKE A PAYMENT NOW
You can pay using your credit card or PayPal.

Auto-billing
The auto billing feature is not currently available. You should pay your bills manually using the button on the left.

Monthly Statements / view full list / view current

Month	Opening bal.	Fees	Payments	Closing bal.	
October 2010	---	$56.89 USD	$49.53 USD N/A		(current month)
September 2010	$6.99 USD	$23.35 USD	$24.16 USD	$6.18 USD	due by 10/15/10
August 2010	$6.84 USD	$19.86 USD	$19.71 USD	$6.99 USD	due by 09/15/10
July 2010	$1.20 USD	$32.10 USD	$26.46 USD	$6.84 USD	due by 08/15/10
June 2010	$9.64 USD	$7.63 USD	$16.07 USD	$1.20 USD	due by 07/15/10

Recent Activity

Date	Description	Activity Type	Payments	Fees
Oct 28	japanese cherry tree listing: 60172842	listing		$0.20 USD
Oct 28	japanese cherry tree transaction: 36624631	transaction		$2.91 USD
Oct 27	rivet series camera 2 keychain.. transaction: 36606499	transaction		$0.65 USD

Your bill page is packed full of information. You can view each month individually for even more details.

Your Etsy Bill > July 2010

This Month's Balance Sheet

Opening Balance:	1.20	Total of your unpaid fees before July
This month's fees:	+ $32.10	Item listings, transactions and showcase fees
Payments & refunds:	- $26.46	Refunds and payments you've made
Closing balance:	= $6.84	Total of your unpaid fees at the end of July

Summary of This Month's Activity

Listing fees:	$3.20
Transaction fees:	+ $25.30
Edit fees:	+ $0.00
Renew fees:	+ $3.60
Renew Expired fees:	+ $0.00
Showcase spots:	+ $0.00
Other (alchemy, etc):	+ $0.00
Fees	= $32.10

Refunds:	$0.00
Payments:	+ $26.46
Payments & Refunds	= $26.46

Applications

The applications section is where you can view the Etsy applications you have allowed to access to your account. These tools help you run your Etsy business.

Add New Item

When you are ready to add a new item to Etsy, this section is where you'll go to do it. Each item must be added one at a time. I will go into much more detail about listing items in Chapter 4. I will teach you everything from proper SEO to pricing your products.

Currently for Sale

This section is where you can view all the items you have for sale. You can sort your items by quantity, price, date listed, and expiration date.

You can also pick the four featured items for your shop. Picking the items you want featured is simple. Just click the star to make it turn green. The green star indicates that particular item is featured. Your featured items will show up at the top of your shop, and they give your buyers a look at your best items. It is always a good idea

Your Account

- 📋 Purchases
- 📝 Feedback
- ❤ Favorites
- 🌐 Public Profile
- 📇 Account
- 📊 Your Bill
- 🔮 Alchemy
- ⚙ Applications

Your Shop

- 🖼 **Items**
  Add New Item
  Currently for Sale
  Inactive Listings
  Expired Listings
  Featured Listings
  Shipping

- 💲 **Orders**
  Sold Orders
  Cancel an Order
  Sales Stats

- 🛠 **Shop Settings**
  Info & Appearance
  Shipping & Payment
  Options

1. Item Info   2. Sort your item   3. Selling Info   4. Images   5. Review & Post

Title
A short, descriptive title works best.

URL Preview
See how your listing title appears in the URL:

www.etsy.com/listing/01234567/my-listing-title

Description
Start with the most important information and provide enough detail for shoppers to feel comfortable buying.

Currently for Sale (52) View your public shop.

Can't find a listing you were editing? View inactive listings.

☐   Renew   ?   Deactivate   ?   Delete

	Title	In Stock	Price	▼ Listed	Expires	Featured	
☐	japanese cherry tree	1	$83.00 USD	Oct. 28, 2010	Feb. 28, 2011	⭐	Edit Promote
☐	Steel Earring Tree - Earring Display Rack	1	$42.00 USD	Oct. 27, 2010	Feb. 27, 2011	⭐	Edit Promote
☐	Simple Necklace Tree - T Bar Display	1	$38.40 USD	Oct. 27, 2010	Feb. 27, 2011	⭐	Edit Promote
☐	Tiny Twig Earring Tree Jewelry Rack	1	$18.00 USD	Oct. 22, 2010	Feb. 22, 2011	⭐	Edit Promote
☐	On Sale Small Earring Tree	1	$27.00 USD	Oct. 22, 2010	Feb. 22, 2011	⭐	Edit Promote
☐	flat round beads	1	$19.00 USD	Oct. 21, 2010	Feb. 21, 2011	⭐	Edit Promote
☐	On Sale Very Tiny Earring Tree - Industrial Construction	1	$6.40 USD	Oct. 20, 2010	Feb. 20, 2011	⭐	Edit Promote
☐	Living Steel Jewelry Tree	1	$95.00 USD	Oct. 20, 2010	Feb. 20, 2011	⭐	Edit Promote

to have more than four items marked as a favorite. When one of your favorite items sells, another will automatically fill its place. When selecting your featured items, look for your best sellers, best-looking items, and even your newest items.

The last column in this section contains the edit button. This is where you will be able to edit your listings. When you edit one of your listings, that particular listing will be temporarily removed from your shop until you are done. You will not be charged the 20-cent listing fee again.

Inactive Listings

Any of your items that are inactive will be found in this section. You can edit, delete, or make any of these items active again.

Inactive Listings (16)

Inactive listings are hidden from shoppers.

	Title	In Stock	Price	▼ Listed	
☐	Modern Time	1	$63.00 usᴅ	Oct. 16, 2008	Edit
☐	Preregistration for Volume 8 of the Handbook to Handmade.......	8	$10.00 usᴅ	Oct. 12, 2008	Edit
☐	Vol 8............2x 2 Ad space for The Handbook to Handmade Vol 8	5	$10.00 usᴅ	Aug. 12, 2008	Edit
☐	japanese cherry tree	1	$83.00 usᴅ	Jul. 7, 2008	Edit
☐	rust	1	$95.00 usᴅ	Jul. 2, 2008	Edit

Expired Listings

When you list an item, your listing will last for four months. After that time is up, your listings will go to the "Expired Listings" section. You can delete or renew your expired listings here. If it seems like a listing disappeared, head to your inactive and expired listings sections; you will most likely find it there.

Expired Listings (36)

Expired listings don't appear anywhere on Etsy. Renew expired listings to sell them.

	Title	In Stock	Price	▼ Expired On	
☐	Holes By Timothy Adam for Artists Exposed for Vicki Diane	1	$19.50 USD	Oct. 7, 2010	Edit
☐	Modern Lines	1	$47.00 USD	Jul. 25, 2010	Edit
☐	Tiny Twig Earring Tree Jewelry Rack	3	$19.50 USD	Apr. 24, 2010	Edit
☐	Holes By Timothy Adam for Artists Exposed for Vicki Diane	8	$19.50 USD	Mar. 15, 2010	Edit
☐	hex steel beads	1	$12.50 USD	Oct. 4, 2009	Edit

Renew | ? | Delete

Featured Listings

Once you have your featured items chosen, you can move them around to get the perfect look for your shop. To reorder your featured listings, simply click the arrows, and the items will move accordingly.

Featured Listings

Want to feature listings you don't see here? Star listings in Currently for Sale.

Title	In Stock	Price	Featured	
These listings appear in the Featured section of Your Shop.				
On Sale Large Earring and Ring Tree - Earring and Ring Display Rack	1	$46.40 USD	☆	▼ down
On Sale Industrial Growth - Earring Tree	1	$14.40 USD	☆	up ▲ ▼ down
On Sale Small Earring and Ring Tree - Earring and Ring Display Rack	1	$38.40 USD	☆	up ▲ ▼ down
On Sale Very Tiny Earring Tree - Industrial Construction	1	$6.40 USD	☆	up ▲ ▼ down
When a listing above sells or expires, the first listing below takes its place.				
Living Steel Jewelry Tree	1	$95.00 USD	☆	up ▲

Shipping

In this section of "Your Etsy," you will be able to apply shipping profiles to all your items. A shipping profile is generalized shipping that you set up. For example, when you are listing all of your crocheted items, you can set a shipping profile with all the details filled in. This will save you time when you are listing numerous items. I will explain shipping profiles and shipping in general in Chapter 4.

Shipping Create or edit Shipping Profiles.

Apply Shipping Profiles to multiple listings.

Title		Price	Shipping Profile
	japanese cherry tree	$83.00 USD	no change
	Steel Earring Tree - Earring Display Rack	$42.00 USD	no change
	Simple Necklace Tree - T Bar Display	$38.40 USD	no change
	Tiny Twig Earring Tree Jewelry Rack	$18.00 USD	no change
	On Sale Small Earring Tree	$27.00 USD	no change
	flat round beads	$19.00 USD	no change
	On Sale Very Tiny Earring Tree - Industrial Construction	$6.40 USD	no change
	Living Steel Jewelry Tree	$95.00 USD	no change
	On Sale Industrial Growth - Earring Tree	$14.40 USD	no change

Sold Orders

When your items sell, the "Sold Orders" section is where you will be able to view invoices and mark whether the item has been shipped. In the far right column, you will see when you received payment when the green check is in the box. You can also sort your orders by month and year.

A great feature about this data is that you can download it all as a comma-separated value (CSV) file that can be imported into most spreadsheet software. The download link is located at the bottom of each page: ''Download this data as a CSV.''

Orders (1627)

Multi-listing orders are grouped together.   Show buyer address and message.

Title		Quantity	Price	▼ Sold On	Buyer	
	twig card holder	1	$27.50 usᴅ $8.50 usᴅ	Aug. 2, 2010		Invoice ☑ got payment ☑ shipped
	Modern Steam	1	$65.00 usᴅ $2.50 usᴅ	Jul. 28, 2010		Invoice ☑ got payment ☑ shipped
	twig card holder	1	$27.50 usᴅ $5.50 usᴅ	Jul. 23, 2010		Invoice ☑ got payment ☑ shipped
	Small Earring Tree	1	$34.00 usᴅ $9.00 usᴅ	Jul. 17, 2010		Invoice ☑ got payment ☑ shipped
	Steel Earring Tree - Earring Display Rack - Reserved for Courtney 1 of 3	1	$45.00 usᴅ $50.00 usᴅ	Jul. 15, 2010		Invoice ☑ got payment ☑ shipped
	Steel Earring Tree - Earring Display Rack - Reserved for Courtney 2 of 3	1	$45.00 usᴅ $0.00 usᴅ			
	Steel Earring Tree - Earring Display Rack - Reserved for Courtney 3 of 3	1	$45.00 usᴅ $0.00 usᴅ			

View orders in [- Month - ▼] [- Year - ▼] [Go]

Cancel Order

This is not actually a section, but an explanation of how to cancel a transaction on Etsy. There will be situations where, as a seller, you will use this option, for example, when a buyer does not pay for the item or if a buyer changes their mind about going through with the purchase. This does not happen that often, but it can.

How do I cancel a void or incomplete transaction or order?

Canceling a void or incomplete transaction or order.

Only a shop owner may cancel a transaction; if you are a buyer who would like to cancel an order, please contact the shop owner directly.

Order — 1 Item				Cancel a transaction
	I Heart Handmade Bumper Stickers (set of 3) Transaction ID 00000000		Subtotal	$3.00 USD
			Shipping	$1.00 USD
	Price $3.00 USD	Shipping $1.00 USD	Quantity 1	Total $4.00 USD

To cancel a transaction or order:

1. Visit *Your Etsy* > *Sold Orders*.
2. Locate the order or transaction you need to cancel. Click the *Invoice* link.
3. In the Order section of the invoice page, click the link that says *Cancel a transaction*.
4. You will then need to fill out a simple form to request cancellation some or all transactions within the order.
5. The cancellation will be finalized within 48 hours, after which, the transaction record will disappear from your *Sold Orders* page. You will receive a notice that your bill has been credited for the applicable fees.

Info and Appearance

Branding and the look of your Etsy shop start here. In this section, you will find your shop announcement, banner, shop sections, and your shop policies. The info and appearance section is where you

Info & Appearance	Sections	Policies

Info & Appearance

About Your Shop

Shop Name
TimothyAdamDesigns　cannot be changed

Opened
February 18, 2007

Shop Info

Shop Title

Handmade modern metal jewelry, furniture, and dis

Shop Announcement

Modern unique metal jewelry, art, furniture, clocks, jewelry displays, and more designed by Timothy Adam.

SHOP POLICIES/PAYMENT METHODS/SHIPPING INFO: http://www.etsy.com /shop_policy.php?user_id=5074716

Preview how your shop homepage will appear in Google search results:

Handmade modern metal jewelry furniture and displays by TimothyAdamDesigns
Modern unique metal jewelry, art, furniture, clocks, jewelry displays, and more designed by Timothy Adam. SHOP POLICIES/PAYMENT METHODS/SHIPPING INFO: http:

Have questions? Learn about how your shop appears on Google.

will set your shop title, shop announcement, banner, and your message to your buyers. Etsy gives you a view of how your shop info will appear on Google. Use this view to help you make your home page look good on Google.

Next are your shop sections. Your sections will help you divide your shop into smaller sections. You can have up to 10 shop sections.

Shop Sections

Sections help shoppers browse your shop and appear in your shop's left navigation.
You can have up to 10. Learn more.

Your Sections Click & drag ⊕ to reorder.		☐	Change Section ▼	Save	
All Items 52		☐		japanese cherry tree Show Off Your Jewelry	$83.00 USD
⊕ Show Off Your Jewelry 10	edit 🗑	☐		Steel Earring Tree - Earring Display Rack Show Off Your Jewelry	$42.00 USD
⊕ Modern Belt Buckles 2	edit 🗑				
⊕ Modern Necklaces 12	edit 🗑	☐		Simple Necklace Tree - T Bar Display Show Off Your Jewelry	$38.40 USD
⊕ Modern Metal Cameras 8	edit 🗑				
⊕ Modern Furniture 7	edit 🗑	☐		Tiny Twig Earring Tree Jewelry Rack Show Off Your Jewelry	$18.00 USD
⊕ Modern Steel Earrings 2	edit 🗑				
⊕ Modern Steampunk 3	edit 🗑	☐		On Sale Small Earring Tree Show Off Your Jewelry	$27.00 USD
⊕ Clocks 1	edit 🗑				
⊕ Steel Beads 2	edit 🗑	☐		flat round beads Steel Beads	$19.00 USD
⊕ Business Card Holders 2	edit 🗑	☐		On Sale Very Tiny Earring Tree - Industrial Construction Show Off Your Jewelry	$6.40 USD
		☐		Living Steel Jewelry Tree Show Off Your Jewelry	$95.00 USD

Your shop policies are the next tab. Here is where you are going to explain to your buyers a number of important policies for your shop.

Shipping and Payment

Setting up your shipping profiles, your payment methods, and your sales tax information can all be done in this section.

Receiving payments on Etsy is simple. The two types that I use and recommend are PayPal and money order. Most buyers use

Shop Policies

Etsy encourages all shops to post policies to help shoppers make informed purchases.
Don't forget! Shop Policies must follow Etsy's DOs and DON'Ts and Terms of Use.
Get ideas on writing shop policies.

Welcome

General information, philosophy, etc.

> Timothy Adam Designs run by Timothy Adam started in 2005. You will find unique
> modern furniture, art, jewelry, displays and much more. Timothy Adam is a self-taught
> metal artist.

Payment

Payment methods, terms, deadlines, taxes, cancellation policy, etc.

> I expect Paypal and money order. Paypal is the fastest way to get your order
> processed.
>
> If you are a first time shopper on Etsy here is a short how to on the check out
> process: http://www.etsy.com/help_guide_checkout.php

Shipping

Shipping methods, upgrades, deadlines, insurance, confirmation, international customs, etc.

Create A New Shipping Profile Need help?

Name This Profile

Item Ships From

Please Select a Country

Country Specific Shipping
Set shipping costs for individual countries.

Please Select a Country   Add

View Regional Shipping Options
Quickly set shipping costs for multiple countries in a predefined region at one time.

Ship to All Other Countries
Use this option if you wish to ship worldwide without setting shipping costs for each country or region.

The "Everywhere Else" shipping cost will be applied for all countries not listed in your Country Specific or Regional Shipping settings
above.

Location	Shipping Cost	If shipped with another item
Everywhere Else	$ 0.00 USD	$ 0.00 USD

 SAVE   Cancel

PayPal because it is safe and secure. If you do accept money orders, don't send your item until you receive the money order.

Setting your sales tax is important, and Etsy makes it simple to do. Under the sales tax tab, you will simply enter the state, province, or country. You can even get as specific as certain zip codes. The nice thing about this is that when you set it, it is applied to all your listings. You will want to do your research on your own location and see what your tax laws are. These change all the time, so it may be good to contact your tax advisor.

Setting up your shipping profiles is quick and easy.

Options

In this section you will find how to set the way your shoppers view your shop, your Alchemy (custom order) message, setting your vacation mode, and your Google Analytics setup.

Vacation mode allows you to set your Etsy shop on vacation, with a message to buyers letting them know when you will return.

Tracking your views and visitors is an important part of running a handmade business on Etsy. If you know where your traffic is coming from, you can better target your advertising efforts. This is where Google Analytics comes in. Google Analytics is a free tool that you can sync up with your Etsy shop to track your traffic.

Here, you will also find a tool that allows you to download your items that are currently for sale. You can open this in spreadsheet software, and use the info as a checklist for art and craft shows and other applications. It is nice to have all your items on paper in tangible, physical form.

Promote

In this section, you will find a few ways to promote your Etsy shop, some free and some not. You will notice that Etsy has a referral system in place. There are no incentives currently in place for referring other people to Etsy, but there are plans for that in the future. Until then, just spread the good word about handmade and Etsy!

One of the questions often asked is "Can you advertise on Etsy?" The answer to that is yes! Etsy provides all its sellers the chance to buy ad space in what they call *showcases*. These spots are designed just for Etsy sellers and their items, and are placed throughout Etsy in prime locations. There are many different showcases to fit all styles of items. Setup is simple, and this system is flawless. Many sellers have had success with running spots in showcases; I have not run one. The benefits of running a showcase spot include increased traffic to your Etsy shop and an increase in favorited items. Items that get favorited by buyers are often purchased later. "Hearting" is Etsy's bookmarking or "favoriting" system for buyers.

Syndication is the partnering with other sources like Google to make your products more visible outside of Etsy. Getting your Etsy syndicated on the Google Product Search is simple. Just click the check box next to the service and hit "Save Changes." You can change this setting any time you want. I highly suggest that you use this service. Google can be the top place where your Etsy traffic comes from, and this is the first step you can take to start getting Google to notice your shop.

The Etsy mini is a nice, well-designed widget that you can place on blogs and web sites. There are two types of Etsy minis that you can build. The first is built out of your own items. You can customize the size and the number of items you want to show. Second, you can show off the items that you have hearted. The Etsy mini is a live widget, so when you update your shop with new items, your mini will be automatically updated as well, no matter where it is. The same goes for your hearted items. If you heart new items, they will show up in the Etsy minis you built.

4

Listing Your First Item

Now that you've learned your way around "Your Etsy" and you have your shop looking the way you want it, it's time to list your first item. Listing an item on Etsy does take some time, but once you get the process down, it will get easier and faster each time. Even though you have your banner, avatar, shop announcement, profile, and shop policies all set up, your items are what will really set the tone for your shop.

When you are selling your items on Etsy, good product photography plays a major part in your shop's success. Product photography should be extremely high on your priority list when it comes to running your Etsy business. When you sell at craft and art shows, your customers are able to pick up and handle your items. Without being able to physically handle your items, your pictures are all your clients have to go by, and they need to be the best they can possibly be. Try to keep your photos detailed, clean and simple, clear, and not too dark. It also helps to take photos from different angles instead of just straight on. You can show five photos for each item, so take advantage of each spot and capture your item from every possible angle. After a shopper looks at all five pictures, they should feel like they have picked up the item, looked it over, and are ready to take it to the cash register and buy!

I asked the some of the top Etsy sellers why good product photography is so important and if they could give a few tips. The following is what I asked them and how they responded:

"Product photography is so important when selling on Etsy; what are your tips for outstanding product photography?"

- Denise Anderson Soap Company says: "I would get a decent camera made for close-up shots and have it cleaned on a regular basis. Natural lighting, for me at least, is very important as well."

- Irene says: "I'm lucky in that once I've created my final print-ready image, my product shot is also ready. But, the following tips can help to improve any product shot:

  ○ Make sure the images are sharp.

  ○ Use simple backgrounds.

  ○ Use soft lighting to avoid harsh shadows. You can shoot outdoors on an overcast day or in shade, use window light, or a light box. Avoid using direct on-camera flash, which creates harsh lighting.

  ○ Edit your image file in a program like Photoshop or Photoshop Elements.

    A simple levels adjustment to increase the dynamic range (from the shadows to the highlights) will dramatically improve your photographs."

- Amber says: "Buy a good camera! I use a Nikon D60 for the photos I take myself. I also have a handful of photographers who do product shots for me when I need them. Every one of those photographers are work-at-home moms just like me."

- Bliss Candles says: "While I still have some photos that I know need work, this is one area that I have greatly improved. My biggest tips are to take advantage of natural light—it makes beautiful photos. A white background really makes items stand out. I love, love, love photos taken at unusual angles or outdoors in a natural setting. When I first started out, I had another Etsian suggest that I put "props" in my photos—sprigs of lavender, cinnamon, etc. Listen to suggestions—I'm so glad I did! One of the best items I ever got for free is my Nikon D40 camera. It takes wonderful photos. If you can get your hands on one of these, the camera alone will make a big difference. When you look at your photos, try to imagine what others will think. Ask yourself if it would make you look at the item. Sometimes an unusual photo is just the ticket to make your item stand out from the pack!''

- Toy Breaker says: "From a buyer's perspective, one really wants to be able to clearly envision what he or she is getting, so the seller must balance being artful in presentation while being very true to the product.

  I try to take some close-ups so the texture can be easily viewed, a long shot (not the first image, as this view is pretty boring visually), buyers really want to see where the print falls in relation to the entire object; the reverse side if it is important to the particular item, and a view of the product being worn on a model. I try to include an image of the tie on a body in as many item listings as possible. I'm pretty attached to those images, as they're usually my friends (and they're always quite handsome!). Unfortunately, I find that the model-view doesn't work as well for selling ties when presented as the main image. If you have well-styled photos, people often don't think that you're selling a product in the photo, rather the photo itself as an art-piece, and this can be confusing in a treasury. I'm sure this is less of an issue for other larger articles of clothing, but accessories can get lost in the whole composition of an outfit or styled location shoot. People need to immediately know what you're selling."

As you can see from what the top sellers on Etsy say about product photography, it is very important. It is also an area in your Etsy business that you should be consistently working on improving. When I look back at the first items I listed on Etsy and compare them to the photographs that I currently have in my shop, it's a wonder that I even sold anything at all when I first started!

Here is the quick rundown of my current product photography process: I have two different setups for shooting my items—one for my jewelry and one for my larger items. When I am shooting my jewelry, I use a light box and a $150 Kodak EasyShare point-and-shoot with six megapixels and a macro setting. A macro setting allows you to clearly get those close-up, detailed shots. This setting is usually represented by a flower icon. A light box is cheap to buy and simple to make. It basically allows you to filter light so you don't have harsh shadows, and it also cuts down on glare from shiny objects. When I use my light box, I use two 500-watt halogen work lights. They are bright, but they also get hot, so be careful!

For my larger items, I use a Nikon digital SLR and utilize more natural light. My larger items will not fit in the tabletop light box, so I have to use light from a window or shoot outside. Just like with the light box setup, you want to stay away from using the flash.

A good tip would be to use a tripod and the self-timer to eliminate any possible shaking. This will take care of any blurriness and cut down on your editing time.

Editing your pictures should be a quick and easy process. You don't want to get too crazy with altering the look of your items. Never remove scratches, dents, blemishes, or anything that will falsely represent your item. I use Picasa to edit all my pictures. It is a free program and has everything you need to make your items look great.

After your pictures are edited, you are ready to list your first item in your shop. To list a new item in your shop, first head over to "Your Etsy." In the right-hand column, you will find the "Add New Item" link. The first step is to give your item a title. The title of your Etsy item is *very* important for search engine optimization (SEO), perhaps even the most important on-page search engine ranking factor.

SeoMoz, Etsy's SEO experts, ran a recent survey taken by 72 top SEO experts. According to this survey, using keywords in your title tag holds the most significant weight when determining a page's search engine ranking.

So, as you can see, once you've determined which keywords to target, the title tag should be the first place to start optimizing for those keywords. Your Etsy title tag is one of the first tags read by the search engine spiders when they crawl your web site. Your Etsy item title is used to identify what the page is about, just like the title of a book.

Where Is the Etsy Title Tag Found?

Your Etsy item title tag is simple to find and edit; it is the title of your item. Your titles can be as long as you would like, but Google looks at only the first 40 characters.

Title
A short, descriptive title works best.

Diamond Plate Belt Buckle

URL Preview
See how your listing title appears in the URL:

www.etsy.com/listing/01234567/diamond-plate-belt-buckle ⟵

Description
Start with the most important information and provide enough detail for shoppers to feel comfortable buying.

When you're editing your item title and description, you can view how your item will look in the Google search.

```
<!DOCTYPE html>
<html xmlns="http://www.w3.org/1999/xhtml" xml:lang="en" lang="en">
<head>
    <title>View Modern Necklaces by TimothyAdamDesigns on Etsy</title>
    <meta name="keywords" content="show off your jewelry, modern belt buckles, modern necklaces, modern metal cameras,
    <meta name="description" content="Looking for Modern Necklaces? Check out our selection of Modern Necklaces at Tir
    <link rel="canonical" href="http://www.etsy.com/shop/TimothyAdamDesigns" />
    <link rel="alternate" type="application/rss+xml" title="RSS" href="http://www.etsy.com/shop/TimothyAdamDesigns/rss

    <!-- provide a check for js support in CSS -->
    <script type="text/javascript" charset="utf-8">document.getElementsByTagName("html")[0].className = "js";</script>
    <link rel="stylesheet" href="/assets/dist/201010221287787458/css/base.css" type="text/css" media="screen">

    <script src="/assets/dist/201010221287787458/js/base.js" type="text/javascript"></script>
```

The last field to fill in here is the materials. If your item was made with specific materials such as wood, metal, yarn, and so on, you will want to list those materials here. Let your buyer know what your item is made of. If you have more than one, just separate them with a comma, and it will show up correctly when you list your item. When you are ready to move on and you think everything looks good, hit the "Next" button in the bottom right corner.

Here is the section where you are going to add the tags for your item. These tags are mainly used in the on-site Etsy search. There are 14 tags you can fill out, and I suggest you use them all. The first tag will be the actual main category that your item will be placed under. In this case, I picked the accessories category for my belt. Just move on down the line and enter the appropriate tags. You want to make sure you are using tags that fit exactly with your item. If you are misusing tags, your item will not be found by the buyers looking for your items. Be creative, and think creatively about your tags. Save one of your tags for your shop name. This will help if someone searches your shop name in the Etsy search.

The next section is where you are going to add your price, shipping information, and a few other bits of information.

Pricing your items can be difficult to master. Be sure to take into consideration your materials, time, and even packaging costs. Remember that Etsy takes a 3.5 percent cut from the sale price of the item. The shipping amount is not added in. If your item costs $10, then Etsy would take 35 cents. Each time you list an item, it will also cost 20 cents for a four-month listing. The total Etsy fees for a $10 item sold on Etsy would be 55 cents.

You can set the quantity here as well. It will cost 20 cents for each item. I like to keep my quantity at one. This way when one of my items sells, I can relist it. Relisting an item on Etsy brings your item closer to the front of the search and can bring in more views. You can also renew an item that has not yet expired; this is called *renewing*.

After you lock down your price and quantity, it is time to put your item in a section of your shop. Etsy sellers are allowed to have 10 shop sections.

When you are naming your shop sections, you want to make sure that they are well defined. You may also want to include a keyword or two. My shop sections tell my buyers exactly what they are looking at. For example, my metal belt buckles are in my Modern Belt Buckles section. Your shop sections can be used to promote your shop and can begin to rank high in Google because they are permanent pages of your shop—that is, until you remove a section. Create sections as you go. You don't want empty sections right off the bat.

Quick promo tip

When you are Tweeting, blogging, or Facebooking, be sure to share links to your shop sections. You will start to build links back to your shop sections and this will move you higher in the Google search ranks. This will also help your buyers see more of your shop at one time. Instead of linking and sending shoppers to one item page, you are sending those shoppers to a specific section, which is a page full of items. They will be more inclined to click around and even see an item they like. This will increase your views, hearts, and even sales.

Shipping

After you pick the shop section for your item, it is time to set your shipping prices. Etsy has made setting up shipping a simple task with two easy methods. Method one is setting up a shipping profile. Shipping profile works well if you have multiple items that are similar. I have a shipping profile set for my necklaces, but not my trees. The reason I use a shipping profile for my necklaces is they are all the same size and fit in the same packaging, so I know the shipping cost for one necklace will be the same for another. My trees, however, come in varying sizes, and one tree may cost more than the other. For my trees, I set the shipping manually.

Shipping your handmade goods, whether nationally or internationally, should not be a scary task. Thinking back to my first sale on Etsy, I remember being both excited and nervous because of shipping. You want your package filled with your handmade items to arrive safely and at the right location. Overcoming the fear of shipping is simple, but some things are learned over time. Here is what some of Etsy's top sellers have to say about shipping:

- Suzanne from Bliss Candles talks about learning as you go:

    As a beginner, you can't help, but have a learning curve until you get a system. Simply put, there are some things you will learn as you go. If you do nothing else, invest in packaging! If you have fragile items, stock up on bubble wrap, paper, peanuts, good-quality boxes (thick boxes—not the USPS freebies), etc. Do not skimp, or you will have breakage—it's inevitable. Even with my overkill on packaging, I will get a damage report on occasion. I am often reminded of the scene in Ace Ventura *where he is posing as a delivery driver—I try to make sure 'that' guy can't break my products. I just did a blog article on shipping, encouraging people to try UPS. Ninety-nine percent of my shipping is done with them now. Their damage rate is much lower,* *and insurance is included. In addition, their tracking is "real time," and their rates are either lower or comparable in my case. They also offer a new Smart Pickup option, where you pay $10 a week and they pick up whenever you ship, even if it is all five days. For me, it is still less to ship with them than USPS, and again, there is insurance included! I never have to tell a customer they should have asked for insurance—it's a beautiful thing.*

- Irene talks about PayPal shipping:

  For a long time, I went to the post office for all my shipping. I got to know my postal people so well, I was bringing them cookies and bagels. Now it's my mail carrier I spoil. Somewhere after year one on Etsy, I discovered PayPal shipping, bought a scale, and never looked back. I now ship everything domestic right from home. I LOVE it. I only get to see my friends at the post office for the international packages, and while I miss their smiling faces, I don't miss the long lines and irritable customers.

- Donna from Birdie Lane also talks about PayPal shipping:

  Use PayPal to pay for and print your shipping labels! Also make use of the USPS "Shipping Assistant." You'll be doing yourself a big favor by eliminating countless time-consuming and costly trips to the post office! Be sure you package your items properly so they don't get damaged in shipping. Even that won't ensure that your package won't be mishandled by some overzealous postal worker, but at least you have the satisfaction of knowing you did what you could, and it will cut down on damage. Now if we could only come up with a surefire fix for lost packages!

- Dennis from the Anderson Soap Company recommends a designated shipping area in your home or office:

  I learned to do my shipping in batches—anywhere between 10 and 35 orders a day. When I first started, I did them one at a time. I also streamlined my shipping, which means I have a designated area where the finished product is, and a table in front of it so I can just pull orders quickly. Also, I would like to add that international shipping is pricey.

- Amber says to keep your shipping prices as low as possible:

  Keep your shipping costs as low as possible. For the most part, the customer does not care about the extra frills if you deliver a quality product. And don't leave out Canada! Twenty-five percent of my business is Canadian, and shipping to Canada is often times less than shipping within the United States.

- Toy Breaker talks about international shipping:

  Have options and don't be afraid of shipping internationally! If you make products that are under four pounds in weight, offer First Class International shipping instead of just Priority or Express, which can be very costly. International shipping never used to be fun, but something we've done anyway since the very beginning. I've been using Endecia (an electronic shipping service) for nearly a year, and it is one of the best shipping changes/business decisions I've ever made. Their nominal monthly fee is worth it times 1,000 for the time and money saved waiting in line at the post office, especially for international packages. Endecia is one of the few ways you can send First Class International parcels without having to visit a postal human. With the continual downsizing of postal services across the United States, many are cutting their office hours, making it nearly impossible for busy folks to use counter-only services. I've also found that being able to fill out customs forms electronically (rather than using the old-fashioned, hand-written ones) speeds up delivery through border crossings. Not sure why, but my rate of loss has also really gone down significantly since using an electronic shipping service. The USPS "Click-n-Ship" free version helps, but at this time doesn't cover all international services like Endecia does.

Uploading Pictures

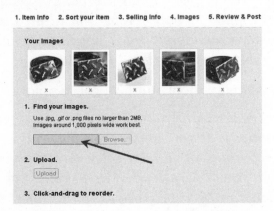

The final step to adding a listing to Etsy is to upload your product photos. Remember: Make sure your pictures are at least 570 pixels square. If they are not, you will see the gray box that your pictures are centered in when your listing is up. This means your buyers will see the gray box as well.

Uploading your pictures is simple; just click the "Browse" button and find the folder where your pictures are located. Fill all the slots with the pictures, and then hit "Upload." This can take a few minutes, depending on how large your pictures are. Etsy gives you five picture slots, and for the best results, you want to use all five. As a seller, your pictures are what sell your products.

Your Images

1. Find your images.
Use .jpg, .gif or .png files no larger than 2MB.
Images around 1,000 pixels wide work best.

[ ] Browse..
[ ] Browse..
[ ] Browse..
[ ] Browse..
[ ] Browse..

2. Upload.
Upload

3. Click-and-drag to reorder.

1. Item Info   2. Sort your item   3. Selling Info   4. Images   5. Review & Post

Previous   Finish

Review Your Listing

This listing will cost a non-refundable fee of $0.20.
By clicking Finish you agree to pay this listing fee.

Your listing will not be live on Etsy until you click Finish. It may take up to 24 hours for newly listed items to appear in Categories and Search.

Diamond Plate Belt Buckle 🖉 edit

$58.00 USD 🖉 edit

🖉 edit

Description 🖉 edit

Check out this steel diamond plate belt buckle. This rugged steel buckle is a great gift for any guy. It is hand cut from 1/8 inch diamond plate. With just a touch of the grinder to make the diamonds pop. You will notice a little rust here and there for the more industrial rustic look. It is finished with a durable clear enamel to protect, cover the rust, and give it a little shine.

Once your pictures are uploaded, they will appear in the slots above the loading area, and you can move them around by clicking and dragging them to the desired position.

Now it is time to preview your uploaded listing. Hit the "Next" button, and you will be taken to the preview and post page.

Here, you will be reminded that when listing an item, you will be charged a nonrefundable 20-cent listing fee. Go through your new listing to check for errors. If you see something that needs to be changed, hit the "Edit" button next to the section. When everything looks good, hit the "Finish" button. Head over to your shop and look for your new listing. Look it over, and look once again for any mistakes. If you do see one, just head to the "Items currently for sale" section and edit your listing.

5

Four-Step Game Plan for More Views

So your brand new listing is up in your shop. You worked hard to make your awesome product, and spent time photographing, pricing, and listing your item on Etsy. Now it's time to get some views, and get your product in front of some potential buyers.

Etsy Forum

Etsy Forum is a vibrant part of the Etsy community. It is packed full of information on selling and running your business. You can also promote your items in the forum. There are two sections that I recommend using for the promotion of your items. The first section is the Critiques section.

In the critiques section of the Etsy Forum, there are many threads where other sellers will critique other shops and items. Try starting your own thread about your newest item. Remember, this is a critique thread, not a promotion thread, so make sure you are asking for advice about your item. Ask the community if your pictures are up to par or even if your price is right. This will bring some views to your item and shop, and it can also help you get a better idea of how you are doing with your listings.

The next section is the Promotion section of the Etsy Forum. The promo section is a fast moving thread with lots of activity.

Critiques

Post a new topic

Title	Author	Posts	Latest Post
Do I need more variety in my photographs?	OneInTheHand	3	2 minutes ago by gingerworld
What's your favorite item in shop above?	heathermarcum	1	2 minutes ago by heathermarcum
Rate the shop above you 1-10	BohemiaJewellery	855	3 minutes ago by lesanche
Needing advice to push shop off the ground	StitchSenseDesigns	4	6 minutes ago by CatherinetteRings
Sale on Sunday, still no payment?	JudeSedai	7	9 minutes ago by skimpysmom
Keep or Toss the BANNER above you.	CreekBedThreads	3418	15 minutes ago by OneInTheHand
Will the shop above you be successful?	PPBoutique710	133	20 minutes ago by JudeSedai
New here and wanting honest advice	threepretties	11	28 minutes ago by skimpysmom
I will critique new and undiscovered shops (under 10 sales)	msaly	120	29 minutes ago by UrbanMoppets
Critique the Newest Listing in the Shop Above You	HomespunHandmaiden	748	39 minutes ago by OneInTheHand
Are my bookmarks priced too high? Or too	CraftyGamerGirl	15	42 minutes ago by

Promotions

Post a new topic

Title	Author	Posts	Latest Post
Want SALES? PROMOTE Your Shop Here. Tuesday 10/26/10	DestinysTreasures	8	27 seconds ago by teaman
October Daily Listing Club - October 26, 2010	serenitysoapworkstx	186	38 seconds ago by CavemanPottery
What are you promoting this afternoon?	teaman	4	40 seconds ago by walkinthewoodsllc
Second Chance BNS - Day 729 *12,263 Sales	sweetthoughtshoppe	271	42 seconds ago by teaman
We Love Vintage! Do You? # 15	MrFilthyRotten	2477	50 seconds ago by JunkDrawerToo
Threadkiller! Win any pendant you choose from my shop!	SunshowerCreations	223	56 seconds ago by jacksescape

There are many opportunities to drop a link to your shop and new items. For the best results, you will want to post in a few of these threads and start one of your own. Start a thread that is titled like this: "Post your newest items." In the body of the thread, ask sellers to post their newest items and be sure to leave a link to your newest item (see following screen shot).

Blogging

Blogging about your new item is a great way to gain some exposure for your new item. I like to post three pictures from my listing and

Promotions   46 posts · 1

Let's see your NEWEST!

SALE
Buy 3   LostRiverRags says:
Get the 4th
FREE!   Brand New
                http://www.etsy.com/listing/59700888/store-wide-sale-hot-speckles-hand-knit

                Store Wide Sale!
                Buy 3 Get 1 FREE Deals.
                www.LostRiverRags.etsy.com

                Posted at 8:58 pm, October 22, 2010 ET - Report this post

                wayfaringmagnolia says:

                20% off

                http://www.etsy.com/listing/59703430/vintage-red-white-
                blue-belt?ref=API_juln_CraftCult

                http://www.etsy.com/listing/59527635/vintage-owl-necklace

tell a little about the item. Make sure you link back to the item in your shop.

Singer Series Necklace Number 67

The Singer Series is a special series made from recycled vintage Singer sewing
machines. In this series, you will find jewelry and sculptures. In the Singer Series I am
trying to capture the character and style that these vintage machines have.

The number 67 necklace is carefully cut from a decorative plate on a vintage singer sewing
machine. This is 100% unique...there will not be another necklace made like the number 67
necklace. Number 67 is clear-coated for protection and shine.

Twitter

Twitter is a great place to post links about your new items. Once you have your blog post written, you will have two links you can promote. When you are promoting your items on Twitter, it is good to try to start conversations. Ask your followers what they think about your new item. The last thing you want to do is start posting tons of links to your Etsy items.

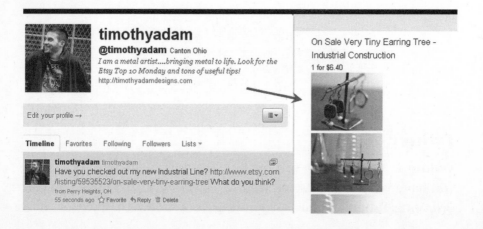

Be sure when you are posting links to your Etsy listings, you are using the full URL address from Etsy. When you do this, there will be pictures of your items embedded directly into Twitter. This is a great way for people to see your items and even give you feedback.

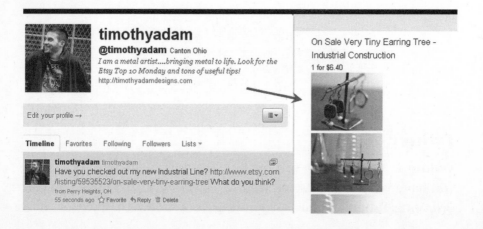

Facebook

Facebook is the last step in the game plan. There are many places you can promote your new items on Facebook. For starters, you can post links to your item on your personal profile. Your personal profile is where your friends and family most likely interact with you. Don't be pushy; just get their opinion. Don't feel bad about posting links to your Etsy items here; your Etsy business is a part of you, and your friends and family should be happy to support you. The second place you can promote your item is on your Facebook fan page. A fan page on Facebook should be the home of your Etsy business on Facebook, so feel free to post away.

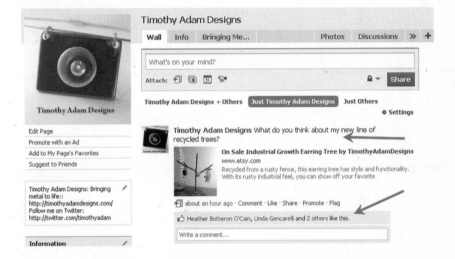

Once again, don't go overboard. Make sure you are engaging your fans in conversation. From your fan page, you can send updates about new items, new product lines, and even sales you are running. You can post pictures, hold events, and even upload videos and pictures. The third place on Facebook you can promote your item is on other fan pages and groups. There are thousands upon thousands of fan pages and groups on Facebook. Find the ones that go with the items you are selling. If you sell jewelry, find some fashion fan pages and groups to join. You can often post links on these pages' walls. As always, don't just post links; rather, engage people in conversation.

6

Advanced SEO for Your Etsy Shop

Search engine optimization (SEO) can be overwhelming at times. Read and apply what you can in the time you have. Don't get stressed out! Being a new seller means you are not set in your ways, and this SEO info can be applied and ingrained in your daily activity faster!

Keyword Research and Placement

Getting your Etsy shop and Etsy items found on Google can be a difficult task. But with the proper research and placement of specific keywords, you can begin to dominate small niches and move up in the Google search. There are a few things you need to keep in mind when you are looking for keywords to use.

When looking for keywords and phrases, shopper intent, search volume, and keyword competition are the three most important factors that determine a good keyword.

Shopper Intent

The most important factor to look at when figuring out the value of a keyword or phrase is intent. When picking a good keyword to analyze, pick words or phrases that people interested in your items would search for. You know your product best. Once you determine what these words and phrases are, use the Google Keyword tool to find more suggested words and analyze them to see if they are worthy of using. I will explain more about this later in this chapter.

Volume

When determining the value of a keyword or phrase, you need to look at the search volume. Are there enough people searching per month for a term on Google to even consider optimizing for it? (The Google Keyword tool provides this info for you.) If you answered yes, then you have to ask yourself if it is possible to rank for that keyword. It will be extremely difficult to rank on Google for a high-volume term such as *garland,* but ranking on Google for lower competition, small-niche, two- to three-word phrases such as *paper garland* is easier to accomplish.

Keyword Competition

A keyword can have a high search volume on Google, but that does not mean it is a good keyword or phrase. You have to know how many competing pages there are according to Google and the competition on Etsy. These two factors can help you determine if you want to use a key phrase or not. I will also cover more about this later in the chapter.

Small Niches Always

Why would you want to focus on a small niche? Smaller niches are searched less on Google every month, but they also have less competition. The smaller amount of competing pages, the better the chance your shop will rank on Google for a particular keyword.

Example

I am going to use one of my *Handmadeology* readers as an example to drill down into the preceding topics.

Kari, owner of The Paper Button, recently started making and selling handmade fabric and paper garland. She asked me about her newest product and what she could improve on. Let's start by doing some keyword research.

The best tool for currently doing keyword research is the Google Keyword tool. It is a powerful tool that provides in-depth and insightful information about keywords and phrases. The key phrase in question in Kari's situation is *paper garland*. Let's jump right in and use the Google Keyword tool.

The following figure shows the results that the Google Keyword Tool provided when *paper garland* was researched.

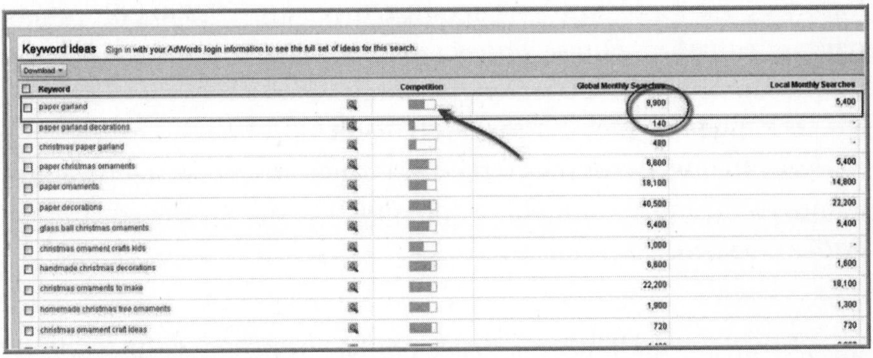

There are two important things to notice here: Competition and Global Monthly Searches.

Competition

In this case, the competition is referring to ad space on the side of the Google search. This really tells you only that other people are placing ads on Google for this key phrase. This is a good thing because it means this phrase is being searched. If there are very low search numbers, then there will most likely be no ad space competition.

Global Monthly Searches

This number is real, hard evidence that you will want to remember about your key phrase. This will tell you how many people are searching this exact key phrase every month.

How to Find the "Real" Competition for Your Keyword or Phrase

Now that we know that the key phrase *paper garland* gets 9,900 searches per month, we have to find out what the competition is. If there is too much competition, this key phrase may not be worth trying to rank on Google for.

Currently, the easiest way to find out what the competition is for a specific keyword or phrase on Google is to search it on Google with quotation marks around the word or phrase. In the following example, you will see that there are 18,200 competing pages for the key phrase *paper garland.* You will also notice the text ads on the side of the Google search.

Let's dig in further to the search results.

Now that we have the Google search up, let's take a look at the competition and see if it will be possible to rank for the key phrase *paper garland.*

- **Shopping results.** The Google shopping results yields only one Etsy shop for the key phrase in the first 10. Ranking in the Google shopping results should be an easy task if the keywords are placed properly throughout one's Etsy shop.

- **Web results.** You will notice in the web results, there are some big-name sites in the top 10 results, like Design*Sponge, eHow, TheFind, and even Martha Stewart, but once again, these can be overcome with the proper techniques.

Before we determine if the key phrase *paper garland* is strong enough to focus on, let's look at Etsy for competition.

It's simple enough to figure out—just head over to Etsy and search your keyword. Make sure you add the quotation marks. This will make your search more specific.

The search results yielded 263 items on Etsy for the term *paper garland.*

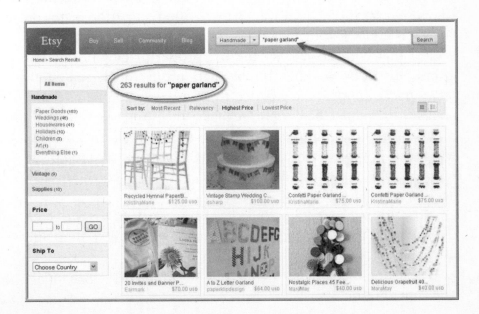

Key Phrase Evaluation

Paper garland

- 9,900 searches per month

- Good Google text ad competition

- 18,200 competing pages on Google

- 1 Etsy shop found in the top 10 on Google shopping

- 1 Etsy shop found in the Google web results

- Top sites like Design*Sponge, eHow, TheFind, and even Martha Stewart in the top 10 Google web results

- 263 results on Etsy

After close evaluation, the key phrase *paper garland* is a strong key phrase and should be focused on.

Why?

Imagine ranking in the top 10 for this key phrase. That means that a good majority of the 9,900 searches are going to come your way. Knowing that there are fewer than 20,000 competing pages on Google is great. Just by looking at the top 10 competing pages, it is clear that with Etsy's SEO and the proper placing of this key phrase, it will be possible to rank high in the Google search for *paper garland.* Also, the fact that there are only 263 items found on Etsy for this specific key phrase makes this strong as well.

Unfortunately, there is no set-in-stone formula for knowing whether a keyword or phrase is strong. You will have to do the research, put all the facts and hard evidence together, and make a decision for yourself.

Now that we have found the key phrase we want to try to rank for, we need to properly place it throughout our Etsy shop and listing.

The listing that is in question is this fabric and paper garland by The Paper Button.

Let's look at this item and place the key phrase in the proper places. We are trying to rank for the key phrase *paper garland.*

The first place you can place your keyword or phrase is in the item title.

Right now as this item sits, its URL is doing nothing for the key phrase we are trying to rank for. In order to have the URL working on our side, we need to change the title around just a bit.

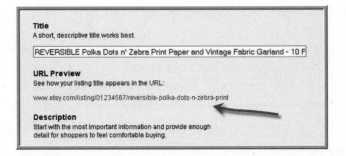

I moved the words around just a bit as you can see in the following figure. Now the key phrase is in the URL. Remember that Google looks at only the first 40 characters, including spaces.

Title
A short, descriptive title works best.

Vintage Fabric and Paper Garland Polka Dots n' Zebra Print - REVERSIBLE - 1C

URL Preview
See how your listing title appears in the URL:

www.etsy.com/listing/01234567/vintage-fabric-and-paper-garland-polka

Description
Start with the most important information and provide enough
detail for shoppers to feel comfortable buying.

Including the keyword or phrase you are trying to rank for in your title also is important when the Google bots are crawling your picture in your Etsy shop. Every picture for each listing has the alt tags already set by Etsy, and the alt tag is your item title. When Google looks at your picture, it will see that this picture belongs with this item due to the alt tag. Make sure your keyword or phrase is in your title.

```
/386616"><img src="http://ny-image0.etsy.com/il 75x75.167/386616.jpg" alt="REVERSIBLE Polka Dots n&#39; Zebra Print Paper and Vintage Fabric Garland - 10 Feet" widt
><img src="http://ny-image1.etsy.com/il 75x75.167/386729.jpg" alt="REVERSIBLE Polka Dots n&#39; Zebra Print Paper and Vintage Fabric Garland - 10 feet" width="75" h
><img src="http://ny-image2.etsy.com/il 75x75.167/386898.jpg" alt="REVERSIBLE Polka Dots n&#39; Zebra Print Paper and Vintage Fabric Garland - 10 Feet" width="75" h
><img src="http://ny-image0.etsy.com/il 75x75.167/387036.jpg" alt="REVERSIBLE Polka Dots n&#39; Zebra Print Paper and Vintage Fabric Garland - 10 Feet" width="75" h
><img src="http://ny-image0.etsy.com/il 75x75.167/387224.jpg" alt="REVERSIBLE Polka Dots n&#39; Zebra Print Paper and Vintage Fabric Garland - 10 Feet" width="75" h
```

Let's move on to the item description. Here, we want the key-word or phrase in the first line of the description. You will notice in the original description that the key phrase is nowhere to be found. In the following figure, you can see in the Google preview that *paper garland* is not present. Let's fix that!

Description
Start with the most important information and provide enough detail for shoppers to feel comfortable buying.

This is a wonderful addition to any room - Would especially be great for decorating your cubicle or dorm room!

Sewn to a vintage Gray bias tape that is 10 feet long. Pouches of grays and black thick card stock are sewn to vintage fabrics. I love how the fabric bunches up a little to look like little pockets! Zebra print, black and white polka-dot, and stone washed prints are used on the fabric side.

Preview how your listing will appear in Google search results.

Vintage Fabric and Paper Garland Polka Dots n Zebra Prin by

This is a wonderful addition to any room - Would especially be great for decorating your cubicle or dorm room! Sewn to a vintage Gray bias tape that is 10 fee

Have questions? Learn about how your listing will appear on Google.

With a few simple changes and not making the item description too jumbled, we optimized the item description. Check out the Google preview. Notice that we now have matching key phrases. This will do two things for your visibility. First, Google will start to rank this item higher in the search for that keyword. Second, this will help the searcher make a better decision when clicking. If you were searching for *paper garland* and saw this Google result, you would click on it, because this is exactly what you were looking for. It also looks clean and tells exactly what the link leads to. There is no guessing on the searcher's side. Seeing twice the results of the key phrase in one search result is powerful.

Description
Start with the most important information and provide enough detail for shoppers to feel comfortable buying.

```
This vintage fabric and paper garland is a wonderful addition
to any room - Would especially be great for decorating your
cubicle or dorm room!

Sewn to a vintage Gray bias tape that is 10 feet long. Pouches
of grays and black thick card stock are sewn to vintage
fabrics. I love how the fabric bunches up a little to look
like little pockets! Zebra print, black and white polka-dot,
and stone washed prints are used on the fabric side.
```

Preview how your listing will appear in Google search results.

Vintage Fabric and Paper Garland Polka Dots n Zebra Prin by

This vintage fabric and paper garland is a wonderful addition to any room - Would especially be great for decorating your cubicle or dorm room! Sewn to a vint

Making a few minor changes in other places in your Etsy shop such as your shop announcement will help improve the look and SEO. By moving the key phrase *paper garland* closer to the front, it will not get cut off by Google and searchers will see it in the results.

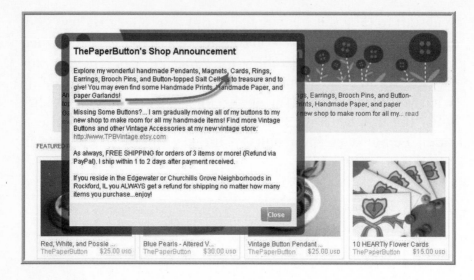

Here is what The Paper Button's shop looks like in Google without the changes made. You can see that the key phrase we are trying to rank for does not show up anywhere.

> Repurposed **Buttons** Wishing Tree Tags & **Paper** by ThePaperButton ☆
> Explore my wonderful handmade Pendants, Magnets, Cards, Rings, Earrings, Brooch
> Pins, and **Button**-topped Salt Cellars to treasure and to give! You.
> www.etsy.com/shop/The**PaperButton** - Cached

You can also move around words in your Etsy shop title. By moving *paper garlands* to the front, it will not change the look of the title much, but it will show in the very beginning of the Google results (see following screen shot).

Increasing Your Google Rank with Quality Backlinks

With all this talk about keywords, I feel I have been leaving out another super-important key to SEO—*backlinks.* I know you have heard the term, but what are backlinks? Backlinks are links on other sites and blogs that are directed toward your shop or blog. Another common term for backlinks is *inbound links.* The

number of backlinks that a site has is one indication of its popularity or importance on Google.

Backlinks are important for SEO because Google gives more credit to sites, Etsy shops, and blogs that have a higher number of quality backlinks. Google will consider these sites, shops, and blogs more relevant than others in the search results for certain keywords.

When Google calculates the relevance of a site or Etsy shop or blog to a particular keyword, it considers the number of quality inbound links to that Etsy site, shop, or blog. So, in our search for backlinks, the number of inbound links is good, but focusing on the quality of the inbound link is more important and is what really matters most.

When Google is looking at a site, Etsy shop, or blog, it is considering the content to determine whether a link is quality. When you have sites linking back to your Etsy shop or blog that have content that is similar, the link is considered relevant. However, if a site links to your shop or blog and is unrelated, it is considered less relevant. The more relevant a site is to your shop or blog, the higher quality the backlink will be in Google's eyes. Find blogs and sites that talk about, on a broad spectrum, handmade, craft, and design, but also dig deeper into your niche. If you are an underwater basket weaver (do people really do that?), finding a blog that writes about weaving baskets underwater and getting them to link to your Etsy shop would be a super-high-quality backlink! Seriously, though, you get what I mean. You know your product best.

Five Tips for Getting High-Quality Relevant Backlinks

1. **Be active in social media.** The more you are spreading your links around Twitter, Facebook, and other social networking sites, the better chance your shop and items will be noticed. On that same note, remember that social networking is a two-way street. Make sure you are sharing the love and linking and post other sellers' work and blog posts. The more you do this, the more people will reciprocate.

2. **Promote your Etsy shop sections.** Your Etsy shop sections are permanent pages in your shop. They are permanent until you delete them or change them. They also have metadata that Google looks at, like keywords, titles, and descriptions.

   Don't fill your shop sections with a bunch of words; it won't make sense to Google. You want it to read right, and so does Google. Look at my example: "Modern Necklaces by Timothy Adam Designs." If you cram a bunch of words in there, it will look unnatural and be less effective. Google ranking depends on many factors, and grammar is one of them.

   Be sure you are spreading your Etsy shop section links around. Also, once you have them set, begin promoting the sections, and do your best not to change them. If you do change them, the time you have spent promoting will be wasted, and even the backlinks will be obsolete.

3. **Blog.** If you are not blogging, start today. The best way to build backlinks to your Etsy shop is on your own blog. You know the content is going to be relevant! Most Etsy sellers blog on Blogger.com.

4. **Strive for quality.** If you are listing quality product on Etsy, and your product photography is outstanding, bloggers will take notice and want to write about you and feature your products. This will also work in the opposite way. If you are blogging about other amazing products, not only will the seller you featured link back to your blog, but people reading may do the same as well.

5. **Get proactive.** Get out there—get your killer product you worked so hard to make in front of bloggers. Most likely, your favorite blogs that you read have a place you can submit your shops, items, blog posts, and even tips. You know the blogs you read, and you know if they are relevant to your Etsy shop or blog.

Conclusion: Backlinks are vital to the growth of your SEO. If you want your Etsy shop or blog to move up in the Google search, seeking out quality backlinks is at the top of the list. Look for blogs and sites that are relevant, strive for quality, get a blog, promote your Etsy shop sections, and be active on social media sites.

7

Handmade Blogging Essentials

I have been blogging for over three years in the handmade scene. I recently just hit the 3.5-million-page view mark for all my combined blogs. And when I started, I didn't even know what the word *blog* meant.

Actually, if it weren't for my wife, Christina, I never would have started. One day, she said, "You should start a blog." I really did not know what a blog was, and it seemed silly to me. I started my blog, and now my blog is one of my top sources of traffic that drives people to my Etsy shop. I never thought that would happen!

Blogging has changed my Etsy business because it's allowed me to connect with so many different people from all walks of life and places from around the world. Blogging isn't just about making sales; it's about creating a dialogue with your readers and customers—a dialogue that will hopefully turn into some sort of a relationship. Relationships will lead to sales and even repeat customers.

Blogging is a powerful tool because it allows you to reflect yourself in a digital world. Think of your blog as your online home. Just like when you invite someone to your home, having someone stop by your blog is very similar.

The ultimate goal is to get each person involved in a conversation and keep them coming back for more. To create conversation, you need to be consistently writing about the things that both you and your audience are interested in. Your blog is about you and your readers. Without readers, you just have words written on a web page that no one will see.

Essentials for Blogging in the Handmade Scene

1. Time Commitment

Here is the bottom line. If you are looking to create a blog that is going to help your online business grow, you are going to have to invest some time. I'm not talking about the time it takes to tweak your blog to make it look good with banners, colors, and widgets. The time you are going to invest is in writing your posts as often as possible. We can talk about all the ways to gain more traffic to your blog (and I will), but if you are not consistently writing three to four times per week, your readers are going to lose interest. For Etsy sellers, posting more than that may be counterproductive. There are other areas of your business you need to focus on. Keep this in mind: you cannot publish a post two days in a row and then skip a week—your readers are looking for your posts and are interested in what you have to say and offer. Think about the blogs you read. If they stop writing for a week, how fast would you drop them from your list? Would you wonder what was going on? Would you forget about that blog?

Putting in the time commitment to create a body of work will also help your blog stand out in the blogosphere and beyond. The handmade scene is growing at a fast pace, which means the number of blogs popping up is increasing, too. Publishing posts on a consistent basis will ensure that your blog will stand out. This will also give you the opportunity to start becoming an authority in your niche.

Blogging consistently will allow Google and other search engines to find your blog. Search engines love blogs. They are content-filled and get ranked high in the search engines—that is, of course, with the proper SEO and keyword placement.

Being consistent also proves to your readers that you are in this for the long haul, which provides reader stickability! This means if you stick around, your readers will, too.

So, at the end of the day, to head down the path toward a successful blog, you have to be committed to writing consistently.

Here are some examples of topics to write about as a handmade blogger:

1. **Talk about your own products.** This is your blog, so talk about your own products. You can talk about new items you have listed, and new products you are working on for the future.

2. **How-tos.** Show your readers how to make something you make. This is one of the most effective posts to write to gain traffic to your blog. A how-to article can quickly turn into a pillar article that will stay around for a long time. Pillar articles stand the test of time, meaning their content is relevant now *and* in the future. Just like the keyword research you have done for your Etsy shop, you can do the same to find out what how-tos and tutorials are being searched for the most on Google.

3. **Feature other artists.** This is a great place to create a reoccurring article series. The features that you do should stick with the overall theme of your products. If you are selling crocheted items, then feature other crochet artists. This is a great opportunity to turn your weekly features into a place where your readers get excited and have to leave a comment to be featured.

4. **Host giveaways.**

5. **Scheduled events.** For example, Wordless Wednesdays, Top 10 Mondays, etc.

6. **Write reviews.** Review another product, shop, or blog.

7. **Interviews.** Interview artists and have them answer your most burning questions about their business/shop/blog.

8. **Links.** Link to other blogs, sites, artists—anything your readers will find interesting.

9. **Lists.** Create lists of favorites, reasons, mistakes, top 10 lists, and questions and answers.

10. **Critiques.** Critique others' blogs, shops, and items.

11. **Upcoming local art and craft shows.**

12. **Art/craft shows you attended.**

Blog topic ideas from the top bloggers in the handmade and design scene include:

- Your favorite recipes/pictures of your home-cooked meals

- Craft tutorials or before-and-after projects

- A photo tour of your studio or workspace

- Pictures from a local craft fair or boutique you've visited

- A story about how you got started making things

- Pictures and the story behind your latest creations

- Craft show or crafty business tips

- A tutorial on a craft

- A crafty book review

- A photo log of a recent trip you took, maybe to a handmade storefront

- How to do a do-it-yourself project

- Before-and-after pictures

- A trend roundup of handmade items

- Other handmade inspired blogs

- Sharing some of what inspires you

- Sharing your workspace

- An interview with a handmade artist

2. Where to Blog—Why Blogger/Blogspot Is a Good Choice for Etsy Sellers

There are many places where you can start your blog, but the blog platform that I have chosen is Blogger.com. It is very user friendly. Whether you are a beginner or a seasoned blogger, it has a lot to offer. For Etsy sellers, Blogger is perfect because it has a low learning curve, and the time spent learning how to use it is minimal.

Starting your your blog on Blogger is simple. To get started, head over to Blogger.com. You will notice that you can with sign in with your Google account, if you have one. If you don't have a Google account, just click on the big orange button that says "Create a Blog."

- Clicking the orange button takes you to the page seen in the figure, where you will be able to create a Google account. The first step asks you to enter any e-mail address. This doesn't have to be a Gmail address; it can be any address. This is the address you will use to log in to Blogger and other

Blogger

① CREATE ACCOUNT ▷ ② NAME BLOG ▷ ③ CHOOSE TEMPLATE

① Create a **Google Account**

Google Accounts

This process will create a Google account that you can use on other Google services. If you already have a Google account perhaps from Gmail, Google Groups, or Orkut, please sign in first

Email address (must already exist)		1	You'll use this address to log in to Blogger and other Google services. We'll never share it with third parties without your permission.
Retype email address		2	Type in your email address again to make sure there are no typos.
Enter a password	Password strength:	3	Must be at least 8 characters long.
Retype password		4	
Display name		5	The name used to sign your blog posts.
Email notifications	☐ Send me feature announcements, advice, and other information to help me get the most out of my blog.		
Birthday			MM/DD/YYYY (e.g. "9/29/2010")
Word Verification	tarnafis	6	Type the characters you see in the picture to the left.
Acceptance of Terms	☐ I accept the Terms of Service	7	Indicate that you have read and understand Blogger's Terms of Service

CONTINUE ➡

Google services. Once you enter your address, you will need to retype it in step 2.

- Step 3 requires you to enter a password that must be eight characters or longer.

- Step 4 asks you to retype your password.

- Step 5 will have you enter the display name you want to show when you are writing a blog post. I recommend using either your real name or your shop name, so your readers know it's you writing.

- Between steps 5 and 6, there is an option box to receive announcements, tips, and other info. You can leave this checked to receive the info, or uncheck if you don't want it.

- Step 6 is just for security reasons and to make sure you are not a robot.

- The last step is to accept the terms. Once your info is all correct, just hit the orange "Continue" bottom at the bottom.

This is where you are going to name your blog and give it an address. Make sure your title and your address (URL) match. You can check the availability of your address by clicking the blue text under the box where you type your address.

When you're starting a blog, you want to be sure to pick a name that flows with your other online venues. For example, my main blog, Timothyadamdesigns, fits with all my other sites.

Another important thing to look for when starting a blog is whether the name is available. The name you want to pick may be available through the blog provider, but you have to check the domain or dot-com. To do this, just go to Godaddy.com or any domain name site. If the dot-com is available you, you may want to snatch it up—this will help in the promotion and branding of your blog.

The next setup in branding your blog is to create a banner that is the same across the board. Again, if you look at my blog and my selling venues, my banner is the same on my blog, Etsy shop, and my web site. This creates a familiar feel for your customers and readers.

3. Promote Your Blog and Get the Word Out for Free

Here is a list of free things that I do to promote my blog.

Twitter

I promote my blog on Twitter. I post links to my pillar articles, features, and blog events like the Top Ten Mondays and so on. The key to posting your newest blog article on Twitter is to make your tweet interactive. Ask your followers if they like the post or what was their favorite part of the article. If you featured multiple artists, ask which one they found most interesting.

Facebook

I will post important relevant articles in the Etsy groups and fan pages on Facebook. I will also find other relevant fan pages to post my articles on. If you are writing about fashion, there are many fashion groups and fan pages that you can join and share your links. Along with posting on other groups and fan pages, make sure you are posting on your own pages. If you have a group, you can send a message, just like an e-mail to your fans. If you have a fan page, you can send an update. There is very little difference between the two, and both are effective in reaching your fans. You can also set up and have your blog RSS feed directly linked to your Facebook fan page, so every time you post a new article, it automatically gets sent to your wall. I like to do this on my own. It gives more flexibility in the timing of everything. If I write a blog post at midnight, as I often do, I really don't want that posted on my

Facebook page just yet. I want to wait until the next morning, when more people will see the post.

Networking Sites and Forums

Networking sites and forums are a great place to spark up conversations about your newly posted articles. Not only will more people see your posts, but you are also building valuable backlinks to your blog, which Google will like! Backlinks help your blog move up in the Google search. Some networking sites even have a place where you can have a blog. It is a good idea to post your articles there, but you have to be careful. Google does not like duplicate information, so I suggest just posting a short blurb about your post and leaving a link back to your original article on your blog.

4. Building a Community on Your Blog

Building a community on your blog is extremely important to keeping readers and generating traffic. Blogs are the perfect place to build social proof. What is social proof? Here is what Wiki has to say about it:

> *Social proof,* also known as *informational social influence,* is a psychological phenomenon that occurs in ambiguous social situations when people are unable to determine the appropriate mode of behavior. Making the assumption that surrounding people possess more knowledge about the situation, they will deem the behavior of others as appropriate or better informed. Since observation of others usually provides only inconclusive information about what behavior is most profitable, the term "informational social influence" is superior. Social influence in general can lead to conformity of large groups of individuals in either correct or mistaken choices, a phenomenon sometimes referred to as herd behavior. Although informational social influence at least in part reflects a rational motive to take into account the

information of others, formal analysis shows that it can cause people to converge too quickly upon a single choice, so that decisions of even large groups of individuals may reflect very little information.

Think of social proof like this: When you are at a craft show either selling of just buying and you see a booth that is crowded with people, do you wonder what everyone is looking at? Does the crowd make you want to go see what that seller has to offer? It works the same way with a blog. When readers see large comment numbers, they want to know what everyone is talking about. Within these posts you can even start to see conversations start to happen. One reader agrees or disagrees with another, and the cycle of conversation begins.

Following is a list of how you can build community on your blog. Create posts that prompt your readers to leave comments. As a reader, seeing a post that has many comments can draw you in to see what everyone is talking about. Make sure you interact with your readers.

Community-Building Post Ideas

Giveaways.   Hosting a giveaway that makes your readers leave a comment is a very effective way to gain comments and community. Having a post with hundreds of comments can build social proof.

Quick giveaway walk-through: There are two types of giveaways you can run. The first is one for your own items. This is always a good idea because you are promoting your own shop. This second is a giveaway for another seller's item. This is also a good idea because you are harnessing the promoting reach of another seller. The best-case scenario is to hold a giveaway with one of your items, and items from multiple sellers. Either way, you want to pick items that your readers are going to be interested in. Give away your best stuff. My giveaways have been most successful when I give away my most popular items. You want your readers and participators to be excited to win. When they are excited to win the prize, they are willing to jump through some hoops for you.

Why hold a giveaway on your blog, and why give away your items? Giveaways start a buzz and get people talking. They send traffic your way that normally may not be there. Holding a giveaway can get your items in front of more eyes in a shorter period of time than most other methods. Giving away your best stuff can result in more traffic, and more customers. If you want to increase your sales you have to get people to visit your shop and see your items.

Getting the most out of your giveaway is important. Yes you will generate traffic to your blog but you also want people to visit your Etsy shop. Remember; get those eyes on your items. The most effective way to get people in your Etsy shop from a giveaway is to require a few things from your participators. This is where the giveaway traffic cycle begins!

Giveaway Traffic Cycle

1. You want to build some social proof on your blog. Comments are the best and fastest way to get this done. Right off the bat, require your participators to leave a comment on the giveaway post on your blog.

FREE MoDErn Steel Necklace GIVEAWAY!

The March Winners have been picked!

Enter your chance to Win a FREE Modern steel necklace from my shop.

~~~To enter: on the top right side of my blog enter your name and e-mail address!~~~~~~

I am giving away FIVE modern steel necklaces each month for the rest of 2008.
The first drawing will be on march 25th. If you enter you will have the chance to win every month.

The winners will have the chance to pick from 10 different styles of necklaces.
check out my shop for all the different types TimothyAdamDesigns

thanks for stopping by:

2. Let's get those people into your Etsy shop. The easiest way is to make the comment they leave be about your shop. Ask them to go visit your shop and pick out their favorite item and leave a comment, telling why they like the item, along with a link to your item. This does two things for you. First, it generates awesome traffic for your Etsy shop; and second, it gives visitors to your blog some links to click on that lead to your shop. Think about this: if Sue is going on and on about one of my necklaces in the comments, then most likely others will want to check out what she is talking about. The giveaway traffic cycle has started.

3. You want to spread the word about your giveaway—right? Why not have your participators do it for you? For requirement 2, have them share your giveaway post on Facebook, Twitter, or even their own blog. You have to give them some options, because not everyone is set up with these sites.

131 comments:

 Inky Productions said...

I really like welded series dots... http://www.etsy.com /view_listing.php?listing_id=13055220 b/c it is so unisex and perfect for gift giving! I always have trouble finding things for my male friends.

I love Fire Engine red for me and I think the swiss cheese holes are awesome. http://www.etsy.com/view_listing.php?listing_id=14186212

September 12, 2008 10:36 PM

timothy said...

Yeah I have sold the welded dots to women and men... oh i thought about painting the red necklace yellow for fun!

September 12, 2008 10:40 PM

 Anna said...

I like that red one. I haven't seen that before. Still, I really, really want that organic steel with the flower. Yep, I love them all, but I'm still in love with that one.

Pick me! Pick me!

September 12, 2008 10:40 PM

elenamary said...

love the "camera" necklace...all your designs are striking!

September 12, 2008 10:42 PM

4. Here is where you want your participants to subscribe to your newsletter or RSS feed. Your readers are on your blog for a reason: they are reading your content, and in this case they are there to participate in a giveaway. The best way to let your readers know that you are posting new content is to provide them a place to subscribe. This can be done through an RSS feed or through a newsletter.

RSS Feed.   Your readers can subscribe to your RSS feed and have it e-mailed directly to them every time you post an update. The following is Wiki's description of RSS:

> *RSS (abbreviation for Really Simple Syndication) is a family of Web feed formats used to publish frequently updated works—such as blog entries, news headlines, audio, and video-in a standardized format. An RSS document (which is called a "feed," "web feed," or "channel") includes full or summarized text, plus metadata such as publishing dates and authorship. Web feeds benefit publishers by letting them syndicate content automatically. They benefit readers who want to subscribe to timely updates from favored web sites or to aggregate feeds from many sites into one place.*

I like to use FeedBurner for my RSS feed. It has loads of great stats and features—and it is free!

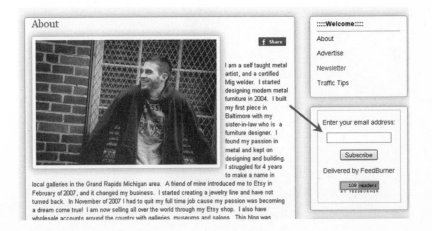

Creating a Newsletter/Mailing List and Harnessing Its Power. Having a newsletter for your readers to subscribe to is a very essential part of running a successful blog. With a newsletter, you can keep your readers and customers up to date with your newest products, sales, and blog posts.

The fastest way to build a mailing list is to host a giveaway. If you have your readers sign up for your mailing list to enter your giveaway, this will build your list quickly. *Bravenet* offers a limited free e-mail system that will allow to start growing your e-mail list.

Newsletter

I have been blogging in the handmade scene for over 3 years. I have recently reached the 1.5 million page view mark with my blogs. As early as 2008, the Etsy community named one of my blog posts **the #1 most helpful post of the year** for helping sellers succeed on Etsy. (Side note – it was a post about boosting your shop's PageRank on Google... Another post about Blogging Success was ranked #10 of the entire year and gathered over 100,000 page views.) My blog has boosted my traffic to my Etsy shop and has resulted in direct sales.

In the Handmade Blogging Blueprint I will cover my top 20 Tips for blogging in the handmade scene. I use these steps everyday to increase my traffic to my blog and my sales in my Etsy shop. In this 20 page blueprint I show you how I, increase my blog traffic and better my SEO with keywords, build social proof, make money from my blog everyday, and much more.

To receive my Handmade Blogging Blueprint for FREE just subscribe to my newsletter via email. Once you do you will receive an email with instructions on how to download your copy. Once you received and read your copy come back and leave a comment!

"Join my Etsy Seller tips newsletter and get a free copy of my Handmade Blogging Blueprint"

handmade blogging blueprint

Name:

Email:

Sign up!

We respect your email privacy

Interviews. Interview top sellers, bloggers, or artists in your niche. Interviews are interesting and give a little peek into another artist's life. Make sure to add a few fun questions to your interview, such as "What are your three favorite movies?" or "What's your favorite snack?" Pick people that are interesting to you, and it will reflect in the quality of questions. The more you are invested in the interview, the better quality it will be, and your interviewee and readers will enjoy it more.

Critiques. Critiques of items, blogs, or other Etsy shops can bring in the readers as well. People like to hear the opinion of others.

I ran a series of critiques on my blog where I would buy an item from an Etsy shop. I asked my readers to leave a link to their shops in the comments in a setup post about a week before I picked the item I was going to buy. Giving yourself a week allows you to spread the word about your upcoming critique and gives your readers and others a chance to post their shop. On these setup posts, you want to tell your readers what you are doing and how they can submit their shop. It's simple and effective social proof building. Once you pick the winning shop, buy the item and let your readers know who the lucky seller was. You can even post a picture and a link to the item. In my item critique series, I did a short video review. I got footage of the packaging and the item itself. You don't have to do a video, but pictures are a must. Pictures show your readers that you are actually following through with a real-life critique. This instills confidence in them the next time an item critique opens up on your blog.

Item critiques do three things for your blog: First, they give you an automatic three posts. Remember, post consistency is important! Second, your readers will start to see you as an authority figure in your niche. Third, they can bring in traffic and consistent readers.

Features. Featuring items and shops will also prompt your readers to leave comments. These types of posts will also prompt the sellers you featured to share your post. They are excited to be featured, and they will share the news.

How do y

I stay t
do is for th
try to stay

How has
helped yo

Oh my
sources fo
no clue ho
gotten to k
be major f

Any spec
want to n

As I so
write from
the numbe
connectio

What is o
to your bl

Most c

Name 10
scene.

Oooh,

1. Write

2. Give a

3. Post a
handn

4. Show

(*continued*)
Do you ma

Yes, I ha
numbers are
from my blo

Tell us a

Hello
born and
Carolina,
ever I am
home and

Why did

The e
and then
share the

Where
writing

Every
ture, and
notebook
me. I kee
time I nee

Who tau
(design,

Ha ha
research a
for me. I'
but have l

(*continued*)

Top Blogger Interviews

5. Show before-and-after pictures.

6. Do a trend roundup of handmade items.

7. Feature other handmade-inspired blogs.

8. Share some of what inspires you.

9. Share your workspace with them.

10. Interview a handmade artist.

How has your blog helped your Etsy shops?

Oh, I would say it's helped from the start. I started both my shops and my blog at the same time, so they have grown and supported each other the whole time!

Name three web sites you couldn't live without.

1. Etsy, of course!

2. Scoutie girl

3. Design*Sponge

Top Blogger Interviews

Design*Sponge

Tell us a little about yourself.

My name is Grace Bonney. I'm 28; live in Brooklyn, New York; and run a design blog called Design*Sponge. I'm an obsessive fabric collector, flea marketer, and lover of all things food related.

Top Blogger Interviews

How did you become interested in design/decorating?

Trading Spaces. Genevieve Gorder's work on the show back in 2000–2002 really influenced me and made me want to design my own furniture and decorate my dorm room. It sort of exploded from there, and I ended up changing my major to fine art and absorbing as much design history information as possible at school.

Why did you start blogging?

For two reasons. First, I wasn't sure how to find my way to my dream job (magazine writing) and my boyfriend (now my husband) suggested I start a blog as a way to get comfortable with my own voice and establish an online portfolio in hopes of submitting it to a magazine one day. I also really needed an outlet to talk about the things I loved. I wasn't seeing the design I liked on TV or in magazines, so I wanted to talk about the things I cared about anywhere I could— and hopefully find a few people who felt the same way.

Where does your inspiration come from when writing articles?

I'm sure most bloggers say this, but everywhere. Online, design shows, student fairs, walks around the city, travel—anything can inspire a post. Usually, what grabs me is a pattern, a color, or a composition that makes me do a double-take. That's almost always grounds for a post.

Who taught you or how did you learn the technical (design, setup, etc.) side to blogging?

I learned the basics from Blogger.com. I set up a free blog there back in 2004 and learned my way around basic HTML by looking at the "HTML" version of the post after I'd written it in the "visual" version. I would compare back and forth

(continued)

(*continued*)

Top Blogger Interviews

until I understood how links, font choices, and spacing worked in code form. I've since gone on to hire different people with designing custom templates, managing our servers, etc. That sort of thing is way beyond my scope of knowledge.

How did you build a community around your blog?

It grew naturally. There weren't many blogs around when I started in 2004, so I think I really lucked out to be in the right place at the right time with the right content. There was no *Domino* magazine or 200 design blogs to choose from. We were all looking for something that spoke to us, and I was fortunate to catch on to that early community; it's grown organically from there. I don't do outreach or press releases, etc. I really believe in letting something grown at its own speed. We've definitely gotten bumps from press stories, but the best—and most lasting—traffic comes from word-of-mouth.

Any specific tips you have for newbie bloggers who want to make it in the blogosphere?

Sure! Focus on finding your unique voice—what makes you you? What interests you that's different from other people? Grab onto that kernel of difference and uniqueness and focus on making that shine on your blog. The easiest way to stand out in a pack is to say or do something different, so focus on finding out what separates you from other people and really work to make that angle the focus of your blog. People always want to hear/read something new and different.

Name three web sites you couldn't live without.

MattBites.com (I love food—it's my other big passion, and Matt is the best food photographer around. And he has such a wonderful, relatable, and genuine voice.)

Top Blogger Interviews

GoFugYourself.com (I love catty celebrity clothing gossip, and Heather and Jessica have a wonderful writing style.)

Ohjoy.blogs.com (Joy was the first blog I started following religiously and is one of the few I still do. She has really found her voice, style, and niche and does it beautifully.)

What are your three favorite Etsy shops and why?

I don't have favorite Etsy shops—they change and pop up so quickly that it's hard to pick just three. I really love artists like Diana Fayt, Alyssa Ettinger, and Karin Eriksson—they all sell their ceramics online at Etsy.

Where do you see your blog in 10 years?

Ten years? Oh man, that's an *eternity* in blog years. My gut reaction is "on the moon," which is clearly laughable, but that's how hard it is to predict web futures. The blog changes so much from year to year, it's impossible for me to predict what it will look like, and if it will even still be in the same form. I'll be close to 40 in 10 years (yikes), so I hope that I've found a way to keep the site feeling fresh and new for me—because if I'm not excited about what I'm doing, I tend to move on. So, hopefully, the site will still be kicking if I've found a way to make it feel fun still.

Top Blogger Interviews

Amy, www.pikaland.com

Tell us a little about yourself.

My name is Amy Ng, and I'm an art and illustration blogger based in Kuala Lumpur, Malaysia. I was an architecture

(continued)

(*continued*)
Top Blogger Interviews

and design magazine editor when I started the Pikaland blog, but I was originally trained as a landscape architect. My love for books prompted me to go into publishing—and it's still an industry that I love, although I now do everything online!

Why did you start blogging?

The blog was started about two years ago, when I found that I was posting on more links to illustrators on my personal blog as I was trying to find my own voice as one. So I set up Pikaland so that I could dedicate my love of illustration and focus on collaborating with artists (because I love organizing and the idea of collaborating!) The site has now evolved to become a place where I connect illustrators with their audience!

Where does your inspiration come from when writing articles?

I usually post articles about new and emerging illustrators and artists, but I also love writing about issues that artists are facing. Subjects like creativity, plagiarism, and thinking out of the box are my favorite topics, as are book reviews that I do periodically on the blog.

Who taught you or how did you learn the technical (design, setup, etc.) side to blogging?

It's all self-taught! Down to the design and coding of the blog. I started by reading up on HTML and CSS, and also used the Textpattern content management system (CMS) to run my web site. They have a great community to help each other out and I've been a loyal user since 2004.

How do you build a community around your blog?

A lot of it is organic growth. I collaborate with artists by inviting them to participate in Pikaland projects. One

Top Blogger Interviews

project, called the PikaPackage Project, is a swap for artists that also functions as a collaborative marketing tool. Another is the Good to Know project, where artists, illustrators, and designers send in advice on certain topics that I compile in a zine.

How have social media like Twitter and Facebook helped your blog grow?

Twitter and Facebook have helped me reach my audience faster. I get a lot of submissions and also announcements via e-mail, and there's no way that I could fit all that into the blog. So I've decided that some contents are best shared through my Facebook page (http://facebook.com/pikapikaland), where it will also stream through Twitter. Dissemination of information happens faster that way and is best to convey messages that are time sensitive. This in turn has helped my blog readership grow, as I leverage different social media sites to convey different information suited for that particular platform.

Any specific tips you have for newbie bloggers who want to make it in the blogosphere?

I think the most important is to enjoy yourself. Starting and maintaining a blog is a time-consuming affair. But if you enjoy the subject matter and love participating in a dialogue with your audience, then it's something you should explore. Focusing on a niche subject also helps tremendously. Just be aware that you might not reap the rewards until very much later!

What is one thing you do that drives the most traffic to your blog?

I don't think there is exactly one thing that drives the most traffic to my blog, but rather a collective effort that

(*continued*)

(*continued*)

Top Blogger Interviews

pays out in the end. Writing articles about my points on creativity and issues that go along with it usually brings a lot of readers to the post, but it's also the whole experience when they're there that makes them want to see more.

Name three web sites you couldn't live without.

1. Etsy.com: A lot of artists use this as a starting point to share their art!

2. Facebook.com: I like to use my Pikaland page to connect with my readers!

3. ffffound.com: I get a lot of inspiration from all the images I see!

Top Blogger Interviews

Cuteable

Where does your inspiration come from when writing articles?

Goodness—it can literally be from anywhere! My children, believe it or not, are a big inspiration. I listen in on their conversations and find things related to fairies, pirates, or whatever they are talking about or drawing. I also like to browse Etsy and Folksy looking for things that might spark off an idea for a post—do the same with Flickr. I also get lots of e-mails from people wanting to share their cute handmade items and some of those can easily give me ideas.

Top Blogger Interviews

Who taught you or how did you learn the technical (design, setup, etc.) side to blogging?

Luckily, the previous owner of Cuteable (we bought it in January 2008) gave me a step-by-step guide to how to use WordPress, as I was only familiar with Blogger. Also, Matt, my husband, is technically minded, so I always ask him if things go wrong/when I need changes made. Luckily, they haven't gone wrong for a while now (touches wood).

How did you build a community around your blog?

I regularly tweet about Cuteable—both about what I have written and sometimes, if inspiration isn't striking, I ask for suggestions about what to blog about. Cuteable on Twitter. I also have a Flickr group where people can add photographs, etc., and I try and visit the Etsy and Folksy forums when I can. Also, I always let the people who have been featured know that they have been featured so that they can pass on the word about Cuteable. Word-of-mouth, really!

Any specific tips you have for newbie bloggers who want to make it in the blogosphere?

Blog regularly—even if that is only once a week. People forget about you if you don't! And be yourself—no one will read a blog if they think you are being phony.

Name three web sites you couldn't live without.

1. Twitter: I'm nearly up to 10,000 tweets on there. Who says I talk too much!

2. Crafts Forum: This has been an invaluable forum to me; lots of advice about crafting and genuinely nice people. I should state that I am a moderator on there!

(continued)

(continued)

Top Blogger Interviews

3. Oodles of blogs: I really can't name them all as I will be here forever, but I love reading about what people have made.

What are your three favorite Etsy shops, and why?

Ooooh, I am going to cheat a little here and have six favorite shops—three from Etsy and three from Folksy. I hope you don't mind!

1. Ric Rac: Just because she makes gorgeous things and is very inventive!

2. Tweed Plush: Because her things are beautifully well made and she is staying close to her roots by using Harris Tweed.

3. PearsonMaron: Take a look and you will see why!

4. CirquedeChaussettes: Quirky and cute circus creatures made from socks! Very well-made with lovely details.

5. LeighShepherdDesigns: Leigh uses fabulous images in her work and is lovely too.

6. Strangelord: Fabulously strange and quirky collages—they are brilliant!

Where do you see your blog in 10 years?

Hopefully, continuing to find gorgeous handmade items that I can share with my readers. Ideally, though, with a few more guest posts, so I can have a little time off!

Top Blogger Interviews

Handmade Evolution

Tell us a little about yourself. What is your Etsy story?

I started out on Etsy as a buyer, and it wasn't until I started volunteering at www.justwork.ca that handmade really took on a new, more special meaning for me. I set up an Etsy shop for them, Justwork, and really got hooked on the Etsy experience as a result. I love posters and origami art, so from there I decided I should start my own shop, Field Trip, where I sell typography posters.

Why did you start blogging?

I think it's been in me for a long time. I started my first "magazine" in grade 5, and since I was 13 or so I've been known to spend all my spare money on magazines and books. Then, this fall, I took the leap and started www .handmadeevolution.com.

Where does your inspiration come from when writing articles?

First and foremost from all the talented artists and designers in the handmade sphere. I'm constantly blown away by their skills and creativity.

Who taught you or how did you learn the technical (design, setup, etc.) side to blogging?

I've been working as a self-taught freelance web and graphic designer for four or so years now, so blogging came fairly easily. My recommendation for someone just starting out would be to get a couple of great books and to try to learn a new skill or two a week. That's what's worked the best for me.

(continued)

(continued)

Top Blogger Interviews

How did you build a community around your blog?

Twitter is the number one way I feel connected to the larger blogging community. Once you get into it, it's a lot of fun!

How does your blog help your Etsy business?

I think by blogging on a daily basis I stay inspired, and it helps me to feel like I'm part of the larger handmade community—which in turn makes me want to create new, better items for my shop.

Any specific tips you have for newbie bloggers who want to make it in the blogosphere?

Not sure that I've "made it" personally! Going with it is realizing that I have something unique to contribute—my own tastes, views and values. What we do as bloggers is important, especially as members of the handmade community. We have an opportunity to influence the culture that surrounds us to think differently about our consumption of material goods and what that means.

Name three web sites you couldn't live without.

1. Youtube.com: Their favorites feature is awesome. Great music keeps me motivated big time.

2. Wikipedia.org: How can you not love it?

3. Scoutiegirl.com: In Tara I've found my e-doppel-ganger. While our blogs are very different, we share so many similarities in terms of vision and personal history—right down to having the same college major and being Virgos. Her site inspires me time and time again.

Top Blogger Interviews

What are your three favorite Etsy shops and why?

1. Irene Suchocki: Her work is stunning and so pretty, yet always tells a story. I have a few prints up next to my desk.

2. Paper Leaves: I just discovered this shop recently, and I am a huge fan of not only Kristen's work, but also her outlook and sense of life purpose.

3. Hine: The best place to get a really cute iPhone case from the sweetest Etsian. Her shop is often only partially stocked, so you have to get items before they sell out.

Top Blogger Interviews

Design Milk

Tell us a little about yourself.

My name is Jaime Derringer, and I am a 30-something blogger/writer/editor/publisher/consultant/artist/designer from New Jersey. I live with my husband, Jordan, and two awesome dogs, Beans and Lulu. We are looking for a house right now. Fun times.

How did you become interested in design/decorating?

I worked my way through college by selling retail furniture. Most customers purchase sofas and chairs, and I just loved helping them mix and match fabrics, place and arrange furniture, measure for their room, etc. I've always

(continued)

(*continued*)
Top Blogger Interviews

been kind of "artsy" and creative, but did not go to school for design. It was a nice outlet, and thus began my love affair with décor.

Why did you start blogging?

I had some personal blogs and an online magazine back in the day, you know, when LiveJournal and Friendster were the social networking web sites. I've wanted to start and run a magazine since I was in grade school and enjoyed writing stories and poems and experimenting. It was a natural progression, especially after I realized how expensive and time consuming magazines were. I knew I could handle a blog all by myself!

Where does your inspiration come from when writing articles?

Mostly from submissions—people send me things left and right. It's pretty overwhelming, and sometimes I feel like there isn't enough time in the day to post about all the amazing things I see. Before I began to get submissions, my blog was primarily me finding cool stuff I liked on the Internet and just posting it as a "note to self." It was a creative outlet that I desperately needed at the time.

Who taught you or how did you learn the technical (design, setup, etc.) side to blogging?

In 2001, I decided I had better teach myself HTML and how to build a web site because I saw where things were headed. I was in the publishing business, which was way behind many other businesses when it came to using the Internet. I eventually learned how to work WordPress and other types of management systems quite well. I still do pretty much everything for my web site (with some help

Top Blogger Interviews

from my tech-savvy brother) from layout and design to ad management. I'm kind of a control freak.

How did you build a community around your blog?

I have no idea. I got lucky. Right time, right place? If you build it, they will come? I don't know, but I am *so very thankful.* I have such great readers, and I am glad they've stuck with me.

I love that you have your blog split in to three sections—Art, Design, and Dog. How did you pick those three sections?

These are my three favorite passions right now, so for me, it was a no-brainer. I have other ideas, but I don't feel the passion and drive for them, so they are not worth my time. I'll only go for the things I feel in my gut and I know I will be able to throw myself into 100 percent. Otherwise, it's not worth it to me.

Any specific tips you have for newbie bloggers who want to make it in the blogosphere?

Be yourself. Don't try to be successful or fake. People will see through you immediately. Talk about what you're passionate about.

Be original. Don't copy another person's idea. Instead, go into a niche where you think there is a real viable need for content. This is what I did with Dog Milk, and the response has been great.

Stick with it and be regular and relevant. Don't quit after a few months if you don't see hundreds of subscribers. Regular and relevant posting will increase reader loyalty. Be patient—becoming successful takes time. I spent three years blogging before I quit my day job to blog full time.

(continued)

(continued)

Top Blogger Interviews

Name three web sites you couldn't live without.

This changes each day, but today it is NOTCOT, Google Reader, and Stat Counter. The last two seem sad, but a lot of my web use is related to work these days! Twitter is also a big one, but I don't actually visit the Twitter web site. I use TweetDeck.

Where do you see your blog in 10 years?

Will blogging even still exist in 10 years? Who knows? We'll just adapt to whatever comes along. Hopefully, we'll still be here in some form or another trying to inspire people and bring them great content.

Top Blogger Interviews

Scoutie Girl

Tell us a little about yourself.

I'm an entrepreneur, a thinker, a mama, and a wife. Right now, my life consists of blogging, microbusiness strategy, digital publishing, and lots of time spent with either a Moleskine or a camera in hand.

Why did you start blogging?

I first started blogging in college. I was a geek and needed an outlet. It wasn't enough to write essays for class; I needed to succumb the whole Internet to it as well. I was immediately hooked and found the money in my nearly nonexistent bank account to purchase all the bells and whistles Xanga had to offer. Unfortunately, some rather odd decisions led to my giving up blogging for about five years. Of course, the

Top Blogger Interviews

whole medium changed fundamentally in that time. When I picked it back up, it was because I was at home with my brand new baby girl and wanted to keep it that way. Again, I needed an outlet, but this time I also need to earn some money. I saw other people making a living at blogging and started a slow but steady march toward that goal.

Where does your inspiration come from when writing articles?

My inspiration comes from all sorts of places. I don't write your typical "how to" or "three ways to blah blah blah" blog. So my inspiration comes from more varied places. I listen to a lot of NPR (National Public Radio), I read a lot of varied news sources, I ingest the thinking of other bloggers—though rarely in my niche. I think back to my college days, and I constantly mine my own life experiences for ideas and revelations.

Who taught you or how did you learn the technical (design, setup, etc.) side to blogging?

I learned the technical side of blogging and web design from the prestigious Internet State University. No, seriously, I'm completely self-taught and self-figured-out. I learn how to do new stuff every day. And I constantly allow myself to be challenged so that I am forced to procure new skills and techniques. It would be easy to be satisfied with my level of knowledge—I've achieved quite a bit. But I constantly want to know how to do things better. All the tools are out there. You can choose to find them and synthesize them, or you can choose to pay someone to help you. Either way is viable as long as you realize there is great value to be invested in both.

(continued)

(continued)

Top Blogger Interviews

How do you build a community around your blog?

Building a community around my blog was difficult. Scoutie Girl had a great reputation before I took the helm in July 2009. However, I had very little vision beyond being a handmade and design blog. As my blogging style matured and my goals for my business grew, I learned that I had to distinguish myself in a very fundamental way. And I learned that I was different in a very fundamental way from the rest of the craft and design blogosphere. So I learned to magnify the differences that already existed: I would write posts that were stories, I would write soapbox articles, I would write funny posts, etc. Soon I learned that the blog had changed and that people were hungry for more of the unique offerings I had. A community was born. Finding out what made me unique and magnifying it really solidified my community. It gave them something to get excited about and latch on to. And it gave me a real opportunity to involve them in the narrative of the blog. I think that's something pretty unique to Scoutie Girl and something I'm very proud of.

How have social media like Twitter and Facebook helped your blog grow?

Well, as a terrifically introverted person, social media allows me the opportunity to be the person I always want to be but never can muster in social situations. And it turns out, people really like that person! Social media has helped me grow my influence tremendously. It's also helped me reach out to peers, colleagues, and mentors to facilitate my growth. Without that platform, I would probably still be working retail.

Top Blogger Interviews

Any specific tips you have for newbie bloggers who want to make it in the blogosphere?

Find your focus. Don't try to copy what others are doing, even in the most well-meaning way. Look at their techniques and their methods, sure, but then do your own thing. Once you've figured out your unique focus, magnify it.

Don't worry about alienating people or creating content that "everyone" might not like. If you are the best *you* you can be, the right people will stick around. But while the right people might stick around, you do have to go out and find them. Introduce yourself, spread your content around, share your ideas, make friends. Don't be afraid to get some readers.

Finally, get yourself "a list" from the very beginning. Think you're not big enough to have an e-mail mailing list? Think again. Your list is the single most important asset your business has. Sign up with an e-mail provider like Mail Chimp or Aweber, create a list, post a form, and start collecting names. Then, don't be afraid to actually send e-mails to your list—it's a natural and powerful extension of blogging.

What is one thing you do that drives the most traffic to your blog?

Guest posting. A great guest post on a major blog can net hundreds of new subscribers and thousands of page views. A recent post on Design*Sponge boosted my traffic by about 2,000 page views in one day and continues to send me traffic, as do my other major guest posts.

(continued)

(continued)

Top Blogger Interviews

Name 10 blog post ideas for a blogger in the hand-made scene.

Come on—don't you have tougher questions than this? Just kidding! How about instead of concrete ideas, I give you my foolproof and ridiculously easy method for coming up with blog posts.

First, grab a friend. It should be a pretty good friend who doesn't mind listening to you geek out a bit. Your husband or wife is probably *not* a good fit for this! Next, have them ask you about what it is that you blog about. Start slow. Maybe just a basic question or two. Answer directly. Then start rambling. As your rambling progresses, go into full on geeking out. Create catch phrases, coin witty aphorisms about your niche. As you're talking, have your friend write down everything that sounds like a blog post—anything that needs clarification, or that you get really excited about, or that you start to rant about, or that just sounds cool. Take those notes and pick out some blog post titles. You'll have more than enough to get you through a couple of months of blogging.

Why should Etsy sellers blog?

Anyone running a business online needs a web site. And blogs make killer web sites. And Etsy sellers should never once delude themselves into thinking that what they have is not a business. Etsy sellers need to blog to build good links back to their shop, to maximize their keywords, to make friends, to form alliances, to document their process, to share what inspires them. Although I'm sure things will eventually change—really, am I sure?—blogging is kind of a perfect 21st-century art form. It allows you to dig deeper into your art and yourself while also providing a wealth of technical benefits to a business owner.

Top Blogger Interviews

Name three web sites you couldn't live without.

OK, this one's hard because, unlike a lot of people, I don't have a daily Internet routine. I don't have a set of web sites I must read before anything else happens. Right now, my web sites I couldn't live without include Chris Guillebeau's The Art of Non-Conformity (http://chrisguillebeau .com), Seth Godin's blog (http://sethgodin.typepad.com), and, of course, Etsy.

Top Blogger Interviews

Design for Mankind

Tell us a little about yourself.

Let's see. I'm originally from a small town in Indiana, then moved to Los Angeles shortly after graduating university. Six years later and I'm back in Indiana, living close to my family. I'm a family girl all the way! Other than that, I love pickles, cheese, and coffee (not necessarily together) and read anything I can get my hands on. Total bookworm.

How did you become interested in design/decorating?

I've always been *very* into decorating, but never really surrounded myself with the right community to foster that sort of love. This sounds crazy, but I always considered home design to be more vanity than anything else—why does it matter how your home looks? But the more I study it, the more I realize that it makes a tremendous impact on your life. When your space is clean, organized, and surrounded by items you love, you're happier. So, to answer

(continued)

(*continued*)
Top Blogger Interviews

your question, I'm sort of a self-taught design junkie. I know what I love (which is a *lot* of different styles!) and simply like to share those things. I consider my love for design as less of a curator/writer and more of a design ambassador—shouting to the rooftops about good design, with plenty of enthusiasm!

Why did you start blogging?

I think the same reason most people started blogging—I needed the creative stimulation, a way to categorize my finds and an outlet in which to explore my community.

Where does your inspiration come from when writing articles?

Oh gracious, everywhere. I wrote an article last week about chalkboard paint because I ran into an old elementary school teacher of mine. I think as a writer, it's key to keep your brain open and present at all times. You really never know what you're going to fall into.

Who taught you or how did you learn the technical (design, setup, etc.) side to blogging?

Oh, I'm fairly blogging illiterate. I taught myself Blogger in like 2003 or something (I've always kept a personal blog for as long as I can remember) and then sort of learned as I went. When it came time to change servers due to traffic issues, I switched to WordPress with the help of a fantastic programmer (Hi, Rob!).

How did you build a community around your blog?

I really threw myself into my blog at the beginning—commenting, making friends, building content. I released a monthly magazine that turned out to be pretty successful, and I think a lot of my readers stuck around because of my

Top Blogger Interviews

dedication to sharing design. I think it always helps to infuse personality into your blog. To this date, the posts that gain the most traffic are ones where I'm a bit more vulnerable and/or personal than the others. Sure, it's a design blog, but essentially, readers are there to sneak a peek at someone else's perspective. Never be afraid of your perspective.

Any specific tips you have for newbie bloggers who want to make it in the blogosphere?

I think blogging is such a saturated market these days that you really have to stand out to make it work. Spend some time thinking about what you're bringing to the table, what you'll do differently, and perhaps even establish an editorial calendar that works for you. Of course, you can't take blogging too seriously, but it does help to approach your work with some level of commitment.

Name three web sites you couldn't live without.

Oooh, I'll always be a die-hard fan of Flickr.com, and I'd be lying if I didn't say Gmail was my saving grace. Beyond that, I love my friend Jeff's web site, Booooooom.com (he's got an eye for all things awesome), and I can't live without KIOSK, my favorite New York shop's site.

What are your three favorite Etsy shops and why?

Hmm, I don't shop Etsy a lot (I'm not much of a spender!), but I do love visiting and seeing new work from my e-friends: The Small Object, Thief and Bandit, and NinaInvorm.

Where do you see your blog in 10 years?

Oh, dear, I have no idea. Will blogging even be around in 10 years? I hope so. Regardless, I always like to think of my blog as a catalyst for other opportunities. I'd love to finally

(continued)

(*continued*)
Top Blogger Interviews

publish my book, or perhaps re-release Mankind Mag in some form. I have a lot of various dreams, but the best part of them is that they sort of revolve around my blog in some fashion. I have so, so much to thank for Design for Mankind and the readers that support the site.

Top Blogger Interviews

Amanda and Jen, Kind Over Matter

Tell us a little about the both of you.

Amanda: Well, I'm one half of the Kind Over Matter team, and I live in western Pennsylvania, where I am a mama to my two-and-a-half-year-old son, Zenin, and we have another little light soon to make his appearance. I am a crafter, poet, lover, and run Pretty Messes and Verve Bath Press, a micropress that publishes handmade chapbooks. I am the author of several of poetry chapbooks including *Love Notes* and *Bloodlines*. You can connect with me through other social media outlets here, but Facebook is the best place to find me.

Jenn: I'm the other half of our dynamic duo. I live in northern Virginia and work for a nonprofit in D.C. doing all things social media and multimedia related. I'm a photographer and writer, alternating between telling stories with photographs and words. I like to help people find the positive in the neutral or negative. Yoga, chai lattes, and sunshine make my heart go pitty-pat, and I think snuggles from my kitten make the world go 'round. The best places to find me are Facebook and Flickr.

Top Blogger Interviews

How did you become interested in the handmade scene?

Amanda: For as long as I can remember, there has always been handmade goodness surrounding me, be it by my mom or grandmothers. All of them have been involved in crocheting, cake decorating, ceramics, jewelry making, sewing, knitting, gardening, so I guess it was the next natural step for me. When I joined Etsy in 2006 I never looked back. I love everything about the handmade scene, the community, the quality of goods, all of it.

Jenn: I found Etsy, I think, through Amanda, and I just fell in love with it. I really like supporting independent artists. I like that pretty much everything on Etsy is handmade, everything is so unique.

Why did you start blogging?

Amanda: I've been blogging for years, via LiveJournal and then Blogger as a personal outlet, a way to express myself and connect with like-minded individuals. Kind Over Matter was something that Jenn and I hardly planned out. I had made some printable cards for Card Drops to put in my shop, passed them along to Jenn, and she suggested we started a Flickr Pool—then that blossomed into a blog very quickly. The response has been so totally amazing and we are so grateful for our readers, their comments and encouragement! Working with Jenn has been so, so awesome, too. I can't think of anyone else that I'd rather work with on Kind Over Matter—we just click so well, very fluid and lax, we are very lucky! Blogging is all about connection and finding and providing inspiration for me.

(*continued*)

(continued)

Top Blogger Interviews

Jenn: Ha ha ha ha. All of my friends had blogs in college, and I started blogging because it looked like so much fun! One thing led to another and I started a journal on LiveJournal, had one for years, and then moved to Blogger not that long ago. I really like using blogs because it lets me connect with people that I would never have met otherwise. I like sharing parts of my story to let people know that they aren't alone in this wonderful messy life.

Where does your inspiration come from when writing articles?

Jenn: Other artists, creatives, and bloggers. Kind Over Matter is very image heavy, and we often feature artwork that is positive and uplifting, blogs, projects, products that we come across that push us to live better or make us feel good.

Who taught you or how did you learn the technical (design, setup, etc) side to blogging?

Amanda: I'm a self-taught blogger. My dad does web design on the side, and I've had a few friends that have tinkered in it, so I've had some influence from them, but mostly I've taught myself how to maneuver HTML, etc. Same goes for graphic design—many hours spent learning Photoshop, which I adore! I am by no means an expert, though, and I am learning new things all the time.

Jenn: I've taken some classes here and there—HTML, Photoshop, things like that, but mostly, I taught myself how to do things. There were (so!) many happy accidents along the way with layouts and such. I pored over HTML tutorials, and when all else failed, I peppered my friends with questions; because they love me, they helped me tidy stuff up. Oh, how they love me.

Top Blogger Interviews

How did you build a community around your blog?

Jenn: It's challenging to build a community; it's hard when you're just starting out. We spent a lot of time basically putting ourselves, this blog, this concept, out there—through Twitter, Facebook, Etsy, connecting with other bloggers, doing collaboration projects. When people e-mailed us, we e-mailed them back; if they left comments, we'd respond. We put our faces and names so readers would see that we're real. We made things personal and intimate, I think, and that's really the only way I know how to make a community. You have to be open and be willing to be open.

Any specific tips you have for newbie handmade bloggers who want to use their blog to grow their handmade business?

Amanda: I think updating daily, maybe even numerous times a day, is something that helps a lot. Find blogs, bloggers that are focusing on the same thing you are and connect with them; you can do that by joining an Etsy Team, too. Read and comment on other blogs. Offer tutorials, freebies, giveaways, make it *fun!* Just be you—you can't go wrong when you do that. Oh, oh! Patience is key; don't give up and don't be afraid to change or go in a different direction when something isn't working for you.

Name three web sites you couldn't live without.

Jenn: Facebook, Flickr, and Etsy.

What are your three favorite Etsy shops, and why?

Amanda: What a *tough* question—I have so many! Jessica Swift's shop: Her artwork is such a huge inspiration to me. Toadstool Soaps: Cheryl has been my soap dealer for years. You must try her Pink Candy and Sugar Cookie

(continued)

(*continued*)
Top Blogger Interviews

soaps—yum! Hydra Heart: I've been dying for a pair of her Keyhole Flats for ages—someday!

Jenn: Ooooh, so hard to choose. Definitely vol25—I love Jess's art; it's so pretty. Lunasa Designs—Rebekah's jewelry is simply amazing! And Jennifer Morris Photo—her photographs are so whimsical and light, they all make me swoon!

Where do you see your blog in 10 years?

Jenn: Ummm, well, we know it will still be on the Internet?! Ha ha ha! No, really, hopefully blogs will still be around and inspiring people. A decade is a really long time in blog years, though, so we'll see what becomes of Kind Over Matter. Hopefully, it will grow over the years. It could morph into something completely different—who knows! We really haven't thought that far ahead but we like to dream big, so watch out!

Top Blogger Interviews

Mallory: Missmalaprop.com

Tell us a little about yourself.

My name is Mallory Whitfield, and I live in New Orleans, Louisiana. I run an online shop and blog known as Miss Malaprop, both of which are dedicated to my handmade and eco-friendly finds.

Why did you start blogging?

I've actually been blogging since 2001 with a personal blog on LiveJournal.com, but I started my blog at Miss

Top Blogger Interviews

Malaprop in 2006 as a way to share my favorite indie artists and handmade finds. I started Miss Malaprop just a year after Hurricane Katrina, and I wanted a place to spotlight the positive things that were happening in my community at the time. I also planned even from the beginning to eventually build up my site to include an online store and a brick-and-mortar retail boutique. (I've made it to the online store—still working my way toward a full boutique!)

Where does your inspiration come from when writing articles?

Anywhere and everywhere. Sometimes I'm lucky, and I have a lot of artists who find me on their own and contact me to let me know about their work. So that's easy. Sometimes I have some idea in mind and I search for handmade goods that fit a certain theme. Lately, I've been trying to think about things that have always inspired me, like certain movies or musicians, and how I can incorporate the world of handmade with those inspirations.

Who taught you or how did you learn the technical (design, setup, etc.) side to blogging?

I learned a lot of basic HTML during my days using LiveJournal. When I first started, there were a few basic themes, and I saw people tweaking them to make them look differently, so I played around and figured out how to make the themes bigger, smaller, different colors. When I moved over to WordPress to create Miss Malaprop, I understood some of the fundamentals and just kept experimenting. When in doubt, a Google search usually answers most of my questions.

(continued)

(*continued*)
Top Blogger Interviews

How do you build a community around your blog?

I think the very nature of my blog, where I try to promote other artists and designers, lends itself to building a community. When I feature someone, I always try to let them know that I've done so. They'll often comment and continue to follow what I do. I also try to comment and follow as many other blogs as possible. When people come to me with questions, I try to help as much as possible, and give back.

How have social media like Twitter and Facebook helped your blog grow?

Twitter and Facebook have made it easier to connect with fellow bloggers as well as fans on another level. It's easier to keep the conversation going and share links to posts and web sites I like. It's created extra ways to get in touch with bloggers and media—as an artist, you can create a casual conversation with a blogger or journalist via Twitter or Facebook without the pressure of writing a full introductory e-mail. Once you've broken the ice through social media, it's easier to reach out to people and then connect on a deeper level and collaborate.

Any specific tips you have for newbie bloggers who want to make it in the blogosphere?

Be humble and try to learn as much as possible, especially in your first year or so. It's gotten to the point recently where it seems like a lot of newbie bloggers expect to have huge traffic or make money from their blogs immediately. It just doesn't happen, unless you're super lucky. Almost any blogger with a huge following who makes a living from their blog worked their butt off to get to that point. Be gracious and try to make genuine connections with other bloggers—link back to them, comment on their blogs, and offer to write guest posts.

Top Blogger Interviews

What is one thing you do that drives the most traffic to your blog?

My main source of traffic is from Google search, so I highly recommend educating yourself in SEO (search engine optimization) basics. I run my blog on WordPress and use the Thesis theme, which are both optimized for search already, but every little bit helps. Also, I try to pay attention to which search terms generate the most traffic to my site, and create more content based on those themes.

Name 10 blog post ideas for a blogger in the handmade scene.

- Your favorite recipes/pictures of your homecooked meals

- Craft tutorials or before-and-after projects

- A photo tour of your studio or workspace

- Pictures from a local craft fair or boutique you've visited

- A story about how you got started making things

- Pictures and the story behind your latest creations

- Craft show or crafty business tips

Tell us a little about your indie shop.

My shop features handmade work by a variety of artists. Currently, about a third of the artists I work with are local and live in either southern Louisiana or southern Mississippi. I've got handmade jewelry, accessories, soap, art, cards, and more. I'm always adding new stuff, and I try to keep it fresh. My aesthetic is clean and modern but still fun and colorful. I work with a lot of artists that embody that spirit as well.

Name three web sites you couldn't live without.

Gmail, Facebook, and Etsy.

Top Blogger Interview Sum-up

Inspiration for writing blog posts can come from anywhere. Movies, music, artists, cool finds around the web, submissions, design shows, student fairs, walks around the city, travel, color, and patterns can all inspire blog posts. Erin, the editor of Design for Mankind says, "I think as a writer, it's key to keep your brain open and present at all times. You really never know what you're going to fall into."

20 Tips Expanded

1. Be Interesting

Make sure you keep your readers' attention with new and fresh info—but be yourself! Having a blog means you have a voice in the niche you are in. As a handmade blogger, we have a voice in the handmade scene. What is the handmade scene? It just means the community of people that are sellers and buyers of handmade items. There are hundreds of thousands of sellers on Etsy alone that make up the handmade scene/community. One of the things that helped jump-start my blog is to start featuring other artists from the handmade community. But I featured artists that interested me. There is no point in spending time writing a blog post about someone's art or handmade items just to get traffic if you they don't interest you. I started featuring other metal artists and furniture designers from Etsy. Stay true to yourself and your readers will come.

2. Get Your Point Across

The coolest, newest-looking blog and your grammar and spelling mean nothing if you're not getting your point across. Have a purpose and stick to it. Find a pattern so your readers will have something to look forward to every week. Make them want to come back for more. You won't be able to get your point across if you have no direction.

3. Keep Your Steam

When you build up some steam, keep it going—press on. Here is the deal about blogging: If you are not consistent, your traffic and readers will leave. When you start to build up some steam, stick with it—run with it. The new *Handmadeology* blog started on August 4, 2010. I am the head editor with eight writers. There are over 400 articles written. *Handmadeology* hit 23,000 unique visitors and 56,000 page views in its first 30 days. This didn't happen because I was lazy and got lucky. No, I built the steam and it is rolling, and as long as I keep at it, it will keep rolling.

4. Keywords

Find out what your readers want to know about, and write about that. Keywords should be the core of your blog. If you research what your audience wants to read about and what is hot in your niche you should write about that. But like I said before, don't stray away from what you are passionate about. Just because you find some keywords that are super hot, don't just write about it if you are just looking for traffic. This lack of passion will show in your writing.

So how do you find strong key words? The first step you should take is to analyze your blog. The best way to analyze your blog to see what your keywords are now is to use the free tool provided on www.webmaster-toolkit.com.

Here is the Keyword Analysis tool. As you can see in the figure, all you have to do is enter your blog URL and hit the "Analyze Keywords." Here is a list of 553 keywords that the tool found that I have been using. Not all of these are good, and not all will bring in traffic.

5. Track Your Stats

Keeping tabs on your stats will show you what techniques are working. Tracking your views on your blog is just as important as having stat tracking for your Etsy shop. Analytics are great because it can teach you *exactly* where you traffic sources are coming from, the sites that are linking to your blog, and a lot of demographics

Here is a list of the words that appear on your page, ranked by frequency.

Found 535 unique words.

Word	Frequency	%
etsy	15	3.35
blog	14	3.16
comments	10	2.41
page	5	1.48
links	5	1.48
tips	5	1.48
timothy	4	1.29
october	4	1.29
posts	4	1.29
commenting	4	1.29
free	4	1.29
post	4	1.29
effective	3	1.11

about your readers. This allows you to specifically target exactly what people like with your blogging messages. I like to use two forms of stat tracking so I can compare. The first is Google Analytics, which is in-depth and super powerful. The second is Stat Counter.com. This site is also free and provides a ton of great info.

Here is a tip for Google Analytics.

Time Trends on Your Blog

Do you want to know what time of day your blog is receiving the most traffic? Google Analytics can provide that information for you. If you already have a Google Analytics account set up and your site is already loaded, just follow these steps!

1. Go to your Dashboard for the site you want to view stats for. I have chosen my Etsy shop as the example, but this works exactly the same for your blog. Find the Visitors tab pointed out by the BIG arrow in the figure!

2. After clicking on the Visitors tab, look below for the Visitor Trending tab. This will bring up the Visitors graph and some different graph options.

3. Next, find and click the Visits option.

4. Next, slide over to the right-hand side of your page. You will notice a nifty little clock. Click it and your graph will change to the time trends!

5. Below your time trend graph, you will see a bar graph. This shows you exactly what time you are getting the most traffic to your site.

6. Celebrate Successes

Talk about your own success and your readers will celebrate with you. Your readers want to know when you have achieved something, whether it be a goal you reached or even being featured on a local TV show like I was a few years back. The handmade community loves to celebrate success with each other so don't be afraid to let your readers know.

Saturday, January 19

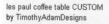

The Grand Opening of Barneys New York in Las Vegas

check out the final resting place for the les paul coffee table.

This is the weekend that the les paul will get exposed to the celebrities...

les paul coffee table CUSTOM
by TimothyAdamDesigns

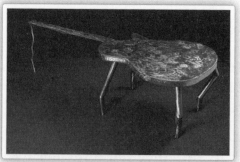

check out these sites for info on who was there and what went down..

My First Huge Sale on Etsy to Barney's New York.

The "S" Project

East Grand Rapids Library "S" Project

Back in december 2007 i was at an art show in East Town. It was a normal show, with a steady flow of people. After lunch Dawn from the East Grand Rapids Library asked me about a custom table. She said they wanted it to be 13 feet long in an S shape. This library has recently been remodeled in a modern decor. I shot her a ball park price on the spot, and i gave her a card. Like most interactions at shows I thought it would be a great project, but it may not pan out. That following monday she called to set up a meeting to chat about the table. We met and drew up a design. After going back and forth trying to decide how to draw the design, i decided to make a small model to present to the board...............Well I got the job and I delivered it last week.....here are the finished pictures:

One of My Favorite Projects!

7. Ask Questions

Learn from questions asked.

8. Poll Your Readers

Ask your readers questions they can weigh in on. Numbers 7 and 8 go together. There are different ways to interact with your readers. One is to ask questions right in a blog post. If you are posting a new item that you just created, show pictures and a little about your process, and ask a question at the end. Ask your readers what they think about your new item. This can help build social proof.

I have found that running polls on your blog will bring in great traffic. You can gain new readers just by posting a poll and promoting it a little on Twitter, Facebook, or even in the Etsy Forum.

9. Comment

Leave comments on other blogs and answer comments on your own blog. Visiting other blogs and leaving comments can really help build an awareness of your blog.

Tara from Scoutie Girl says:

> But one thing that never fails is writing an awesome comment. Not a "that's great!" or "those are beautiful!" kind of comment, but a comment that adds to my post. If all I do is write or curate beautiful posts, my blog is less than it could be. When you add to the conversation, when you bring something to the table that wasn't there before, you make my blog better. A lot better. I keep this in mind when I comment on blogs, too. And I think it works. Even if I don't get a link, I'm much more likely to get a new friend, someone who will be interested in me as a person and someone who will be there when I need a favor. That's community building in the blogosphere.

10. It's Not about You

Your blog is about your readers. Wait! I did say that your blog should be about what you like and what you are passionate about. There is a fine line there that you have to discover. You have to know what your readers want to know and read about. Ask them questions about your blog. Ask them what they want to see next. Give them options that you like and let them pick from the list. I run a poll on one of my fan pages that asks what you want to know more about. This is a great way to find out what your readers are looking for!

11. Keep on Tweaking

Keep things fresh and new. Make sure you are up on the latest in the blogging world. Be sure you are keeping thing up to date.

12. Be Different

You have to stand out in the crowd, so do something different. Look at what other bloggers are doing and come up with something different. Use that creative mind!

13. Interview

Look for other bloggers and artists. Interviews are a great way to provide killer content and at the same time build traffic. When you interview other people, whether it be a fellow artist or even a big time seller on Etsy, you will gain traffic. People are interested in the process of an artist. Take the Etsy featured artist, for example. When you interview someone in the handmade community, they will promote and send traffic to your blog. They are excited and they want they friends, buyers, and followers to see where they are featured. The more you give back, the more others will be interested in interviewing you.

14. Guest Blog

Another way to start growing readership on your blog is to guest blog on other blogs. This may sound strange, but if you are writing on a more popular blog and writing good-quality posts, then the readers will want to check out your blog to see what is happening in your world. Look for blogs with more traffic and more readers. You will also want to make sure the blogs you are looking at fit with your writing style and niche.

15. Take on Guest Bloggers

One great way to add more content to your blog is to take on guest bloggers. Put the word out that you are looking for a few guest bloggers. Guest bloggers are great because they already have a readership, and when they guest write for you, they will spread the word. Make sure you spell out what exactly you need from writers and explain to them the direction of your blog.

16. Monetize your Blog—Make Daily Income from Your Blog

The easiest way to make a little income from your blog is using ProjectWonderful.com. Project Wonderful is an online advertising broker with an innovative model that brings fairness, transparency, and profitability to the advertising process. The first step is to create an account and load an ad. Once you have this done, you are ready to start an ad campaign. I suggest that you get familiar with running some ads on PW before you start to add them to your blog.

PW Question and Answer

Q. **HelenesDreams**—I keep getting e-mails that I am outbid here or there, and I find that I honestly do not have time to log in and mess around with trying to place bids every single day. Is there a way to defeat this? I need affordable advertising, but this one-cent thing starts to feel like a game of some sort.

A. **TimothyAdamDesigns**—Using the campaign option of PW is a great way to set it and forget it. If you follow the basic steps outlined in the video, you will not have to worry about placing bids every day. When you are using the campaign option, the annoying e-mails won't be sent. I recommend trying a campaign. You can always cancel it if you think it is not being effective.

Q. **beadifulbaublesSC**—Is there a number as far as averages go that connects views to purchases through PW? Because some say they get 500+ views per day, but views does not always equal sales.

A. TimothyAdamDesigns—Oh, wouldn't that be nice. We have no way to track direct sales from PW. Until Etsy starts providing us with those types of shop stats, we are in the dark about a ton of great info. Google Analytics can tell you a great deal of information, but not exactly where a sale came from.

Q. JessicaC—My question would be how many actual targeted views should I be expected to get?

A. TimothyAdamDesigns—With the campaign system, you are targeting a specific target audience. If you sell soap, you won't want to advertise on a car site—well, maybe you would; those guys are dirty! You get what I mean—when you can target your audience, take advantage and DO IT!

Q. bobnstitch—How do I know it is working and worth the money?

A. TimothyAdamDesigns—With the powerful stats that PW provides, you will know every 30 minutes if your ads are worth it. You may not know if the views are turning into sales in the short term, but track your ad campaigns long term and you will notice the difference.

Q. Waterrose—I would be curious to know if buying for just a couple of days gets results. I'm thinking that running a campaign for a couple of months, since the costs are usually pretty low, makes the most sense.

A. TimothyAdamDesigns—I like to run ads for about a week. That way, I am spreading my ads out over a broad spectrum. I have seen great results in running campaigns for only a few days.

(continued)

(continued)

Q. TheBrassHussy—I'd like to know your opinion on the value of a $0.01 click, versus a $1.00 click.

A. TimothyAdamDesigns—I have advertised on sites ranging from free to $15 per day. I have found that the best bang for your buck is running campaigns on the lower-priced ads. Sure, you can get lots of page views for the $15 ads, but that still does not guarantee the clicks, so why not diversify over hundreds of sites.

Q. bondagetea—What type of graphics work best as ads? Animated? Text only? Text + picture? Picture only? Should we advertise our shop (using our logo, avatar, something recognizable as representing the creator or online presence as a whole) or specific products? Does it depend on where we advertise?

A. TimothyAdamDesigns The animated ads are the best and most effective. With an animated gif ad, you can display more than one pic! I would advertise your entire shop or a section in your shop. If you are using a single product, when it sells, the page will no longer be there. When you are using your entire shop or section, the page will never change.

17. Use Twitter and Facebook

Connect and learn from others and drive traffic to your blog. Using Twitter and Facebook to drive traffic to your blog is the most effective for me. The first step to using Twitter to promote your blog is to add a "Retweet" button to all of your posts. The greatest thing about Facebook is its viral nature. When one person sees something that they like, they can share that, and so on and so on. This makes links so much more powerful on Facebook. Be sure when people comment on a wall post that you comment back. You will begin to create a community!

18. Be Consistent

Post five to six times per week.

19. Be Committed

You know what I mean! Here is the bottom line. If you are looking to create a blog that is going to help your online business grow, you are going to have to invest some time. I not talking about the time it takes to tweak your blog to make it look good, with banners, colors, and widgets. The time you are going to invest is in writing your posts as often as possible. We can talk about all the ways to gain more traffic to your blog, but if you are not consistently writing five to six times per week, your readers are going to lose interest. You cannot publish a post two days in a row and skip a week—your readers are looking for your posts and are interested in what you have to say and offer. Think about the blogs you read. If they stopped writing for a week, how fast would you drop them from your list?

Putting in the time commitment to create a body of work will also help your blog stand out in the blogosphere and beyond. This will allow Google and other search engines to find your blog—and this will also prove to your readers that you are in this for the long haul, which provides stickability!

So, at the end of the day, to head down the path toward a successful blog, you have to be committed to writing consistently. The number of handmade blogs is growing at an insane pace, so you have to stand out!

20. Have Fun

If you are not having fun, it's not worth it. Find out how to bring the fun back!

8

Twitter for Etsy Sellers

Twitter is a powerful tool for promoting your Etsy shop. Here are some terms and their definitions to help you understand Twitter a little better.

Basic Twitter Terms You Should Know

Tweet: This is an update that you send out. It must always be less than 140 characters. In the 140 characters, every letter and space is counted, so plan out your tweets to pack in the most info. You can include links, and now with the "New Twitter," pictures and videos are embedded right into the conversation. This is a great way to show off your Etsy items because, as you know, pictures sell your products.

@Reply: When you want to reply to a tweet that someone sends and you don't mind if the world sees it, use "@username—The rest of the messages goes here." This allows the other user to know that you're responding to their tweet. And it lets your followers know who you are talking to and what you are talking about. Like I said, it's public. It's very similar to writing on someone's wall on Facebook. The reply starts the conversation and keeps it going.

Direct messages (DMs): If you don't want the message to be open to the public, send a direct message to the other person.

The direct message works just like an e-mail and still has to be kept short. The 140-character limit applies here, too.

Hashtags: These are used to track conversations. For example, if you are at a craft show or conference, there might be a specific hashtag for that event. It would look like this: "#conference." That way you know whenever someone uses that in their tweet, they are referring to a specific conversation.

Retweet: If you see someone type a message that says, "RT @timothyadam—The last messages timothyadam mentioned goes here." Retweeting happens when someone finds a tweet of particular value or usefulness and they want to share the tweet with their readers. This way you can share the tweet and still give the original writer credit for it.

Follow Friday: Every Friday on Twitter, people like to give shout-outs to people they like to follow. The hashtag for Follow Friday looks like this: #followfriday.

URL shorteners: Due to the 140-character limit of each of your tweets, you may find it difficult to include full URLs in a message. Most URLs are long and could even fill the entire 140 characters. There are many services that can take those long URLs and turn them into a shorter one that is usually under 20 characters.

Fail Whale: Not truly a technical Twitter term, but it refers to the picture of the whale that appears on the screen when Twitter is having issues.

Aplusk: You may run into this term from time to time. This is Ashton Kutcher's Twitter name.

Twitter lists: These lists are put together by users to group like-minded people together. Lists give you the ability to sort through followers and read tweets that are important to you.

Quick Twitter Overview

Twitter is not a difficult site to understand. Here are a few tips and tricks that will help you build your following and promote your Etsy shop.

Twitter is first and foremost a social networking site, which means it is designed with conversation and connecting in mind. Twitter, however, is ever changing with the times, and can be an effective tool for marketing your Etsy shop as well. There is a line between social networking and social marketing, and Twitter is a great place to combine the two.

You are allowed only 140 characters in a Twitter update, so this is where your creativity will come into play. The reason you are allowed only 140 characters is that, from the very beginning, Twitter was designed for short updates to let your friends know what you are up to. The 140-character allowance was a new concept in the social networking scene; people loved it and it stuck.

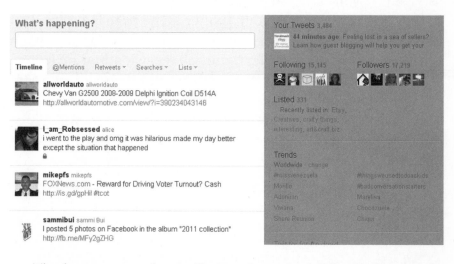

The home page of your Twitter is packed full of information. To start off, you will see your timeline. This is where you are going to see all the tweets from the people you are following. In this timeline you will be able to interact with your followers in a number of ways. First, you will be able to reply and start conversations, and also retweet exactly what people tweet. In the Timeline tab, you will be able to view pictures and videos if your followers have them embedded in their tweets. You can also expand and see the conversations between you and your followers.

The second tab includes all the times someone has mentioned or @replied you in a tweet. This is where you can see who is talking about you. Again, you can reply, retweet, and view embedded media here.

The third tab includes all the retweets that you and your followers are tweeting. This is a great way to keep tabs on what is being spread around Twitter.

The fourth tab is for your searches. When you search a certain word, phrase, or hashtag, you can save that search and come back to it. For example, if you want to find out who is talking about jewelry today on Twitter, just type *jewelry* in the search bar. You will get results and be asked if you want to save the search.

The last tab is the list tab. Here you will be able to create new lists, and view the lists you have already created.

The right-hand side of your Twitter home page is also packed full of info. Starting from the top, the first piece of info you will see is your most recent tweet. Next, you will see whom you are following and who follows you. You can expand these to see them all. After your followers, you will see the lists you are listed in. This also expands, so you can view all the lists. Finally, you will notice the trending topics on Twitter. Check out these topics to keep informed about what people are talking about on Twitter.

9

Facebook for Handmade

Facebook has literally changed the lives of millions of people. It has changed the way we view the world and will continue to evolve and shape what we do.

Facebook is a very powerful tool. Consider this: after teaching one lady about how to use Facebook, she told me that she signed up for the site and found her best friend from college who she hadn't spoken to in over 30 years!

And that is what makes Facebook so great—right? Ten years ago, if you lost a friend's contact information, how would you reach them? If you didn't have their address, you couldn't send them mail. If you didn't have their phone number, there was no way to call. Few people had cell phones. Looking up contact information required a phone book—you couldn't just get online.

But now everything has changed. If I need someone's contact information, I'll be able to find it, either through some sort of social network or through Google. There *will* be a way to find them.

Unfortunately, most people don't search for your Etsy shop like they search for an old friend. This is why it is *so* important to learn how to market your products online.

How many times have you seen a not-so-good product have a whole bunch of sales? And you wonder, "If that product is selling, why isn't *mine?!*"

I know exactly how you feel, and I'm hoping that, after you read this book, you won't have that problem.

So let's get started.

Facebook Stats

- Facebook has more than 200 million active users.

- More than 100 million users log on to Facebook at least once each day.

- More than two-thirds of Facebook users are outside of college.

- The fastest growing demographic is *women* over the age of 55.

- The average user has 120 friends on the site.

- More than 3.5 billion minutes are spent on Facebook each day (worldwide).

- More than 20 million users update their statuses at least once each day.

- More than 4 million users become fans of pages each day.

Before you start finding your friends on Facebook, you need to set up your personal profile page correctly.

- When setting up your profile page, you need to use your own name. Facebook is built around the connections with people, and using your name instead of your Etsy shop name will benefit you in the long run. Not using your name could also result in your account's being shut down—and we don't want that.

- Next, you want to pick your profile picture. Once again, this is for your profile, so make sure when you pick pictures, they are of you and not your logo or products.

- Start adding your personal brand to your Facebook profile page.

Facebook Terms

Wall: The wall is the center of your profile for adding new things, like photos, videos, notes, and other application content.

The publisher at the top of your wall allows you to update your status and share content through many different kinds of wall posts. You can also add content to your friends' walls by using the publisher box that appears at the top of their profiles.

Status: This is a short update about what you are doing at that very moment. By default, your friends and people in your networks can see your status. You can restrict this further from the profile section of the Privacy page.

Boxes tab: The Boxes tab is the home for all of your applications. Applications are a core part of the Facebook experience, and the Boxes tab allows you to keep all of your added applications in a single, organized space. If there are specific applications that you really like and want to feature on your profile, you can add them to your wall and Info tab. You can feature three applications in this column; the column will appear identically when viewing either the Wall or Info tab. To do so, click the pencil icon on an application box and select "Move to Wall tab."

You can also create a specific tab dedicated to an application. To do so, click the "+" icon at the top of the tabs on your profile. You will then be able to select an application from the menu that appears and create a dedicated tab for that application.

Fan page: A public figure, business, or brand can create a Facebook page to share information, interact with their fans, and create a highly engaging presence on Facebook. Pages are distinct presences that are optimized to represent a business and are separate from user profiles. Like profiles, they can be enhanced with applications that help the organization communicate with and engage their fans, and capture new audiences virally through their fans' recommendations to their friends. More than 3 million users become fans of Facebook pages every day.

You can easily use your personal account to manage a Facebook page for your organization. Please note that only the official representative of an organization is permitted to create a page; "fan" pages are not permitted and will be removed.

Fan Page versus Personal Profile

Each user is permitted to maintain a single account, which is represented by a profile. Profiles can be used only to represent an individual, and must be held under an individual name. This account can also be used to manage multiple Facebook pages that represent businesses or other organizations. You may only create Facebook pages to represent real organizations of which you are an authorized representative, and fans of these pages won't be able to see that you are the page admin, or have any access to your personal account.

All personal site features, such as friending and messaging, are also for personal use only and may not be used for professional promotion. If you add a user as a friend, for example, this person will be invited to be a friend of your profile and not your page. Using personal site features for professional promotion or creating unauthorized pages may result in your account being warned or disabled.

Fan Page versus Facebook Groups

Pages can be created only to represent a real public figure, artist, brand, or organization, and may be created only by an official representative of that entity. Groups can be created by any user and about any topic, as a space for users to share their opinions and interest in that subject. Pages can be customized with rich media and interactive applications to engage page visitors. Applications can't be added to groups.

Pages are designed to allow page admins to maintain a personal/professional distinction on Facebook, while groups are a part of your personal Facebook experience. If you're a group admin, your name will appear on that group, while pages will never display their admin's names. Additionally, when you take actions on your group, such as posting on your group's wall, these actions will appear to come from you as an individual. However, if you post or take other actions on a page you own, it will appear to come from the page.

As long as a group is under 5,000 members, group admins can send messages to the group members that will appear in their inboxes. If the group exceeds 5,000, admins can't send messages to all members. Page admins can send updates to fans through the page, and these updates will appear in the ''Updates'' section of fans' inboxes. There is no limit on how many fans you may send an update to, or how many total fans a page can have. It's also possible to restrict access to a group, so that new members have to be approved, but access to a page can be restricted only by certain ages and locations.

Basic

Before you start finding your friends on Facebook, you need to set up your personal profile page correctly.

- When setting up your profile page, you need to use your own name. Facebook is built around the connections with people, and using your name instead of your Etsy shop name will benefit you in the long run. Not using your name could also result in your account's being shut down—and we don't want that.

- Next, you want to pick your profile picture. Once again, this is for your profile, so make sure when you pick pictures, they are of you and not your logo or products.

- Start adding your personal brand to your Facebook profile page.

Once you have your profile up and running, you will want to enter all your information. You can find your information under your avatar. Just click the ''Edit'' button.

Fill out your info page! You can add all the sites you want. Add links to your fan pages and even your Twitter.

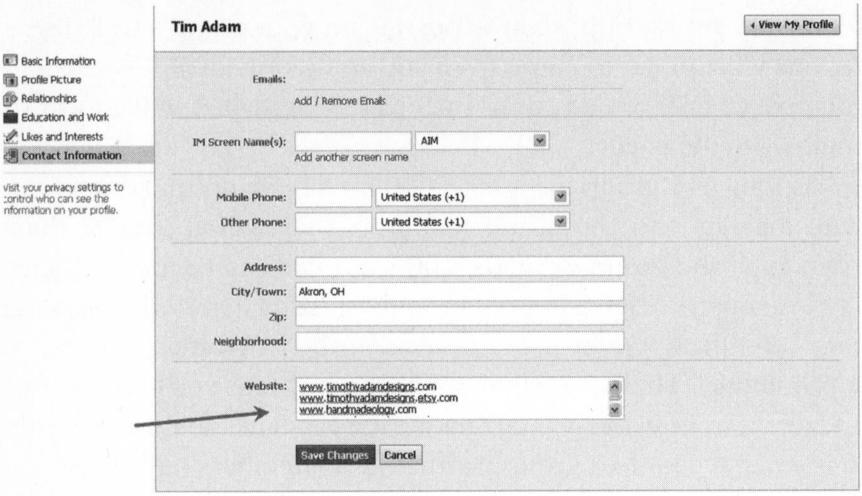

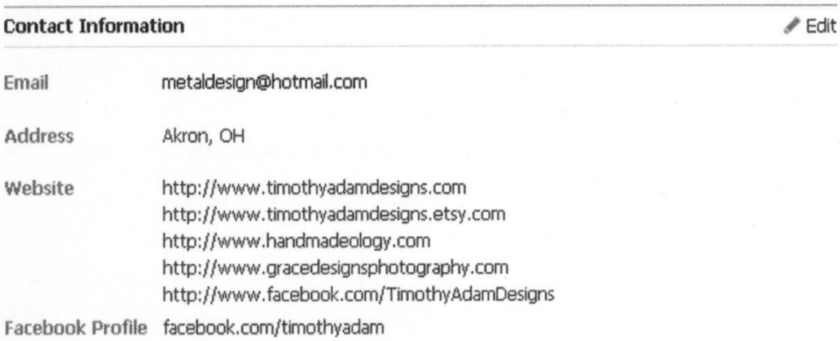

Another place to add a link to your web site or Etsy shop is in the info box shown in the following figure. You can add more info about you and other web sites, too.

Facebook is so viral because anytime you do some sort of activity online, your entire network of friends is notified.

Think about this: Let's say you have 100 friends on Facebook. When you share a link to an article you wrote on your blog, your friends can comment on that. If 10 out of 100 of your friends like or comment on your link, it will show up on those 10 friends' walls so all their friends can see it. If those people like it, they can spread it, and so on. This process can spread like wildfire, and that link could be seen by thousands of people before you know it.

Fan Page Info

A Facebook fan page is a customizable presence for your Etsy shop to join the conversation with Facebook users. The page focuses on the stream of your content posted by and controlled by you. By leveraging the real connections between friends on Facebook, a fan page lets fans become advocates of your Etsy shop and brand. Posts by you will start to appear in news feeds, giving fan pages a stronger voice to reach their fans.

More people can find out about your business because your fan page gets indexed and is searchable inside and outside of Facebook. Other reasons include:

- The **number of fans you can have is unlimited** (whereas the friend limit is 5,000).

- Activity on your page helps increase what I call "**viral visibility**" on Facebook.

- You can **establish your brand** even further.

Setting Up your Facebook Fan Page

First things first. You need to find the page where you can set up your very own fan/business page. You can find the link at the bottom of any fan page noted in the following screen shot.

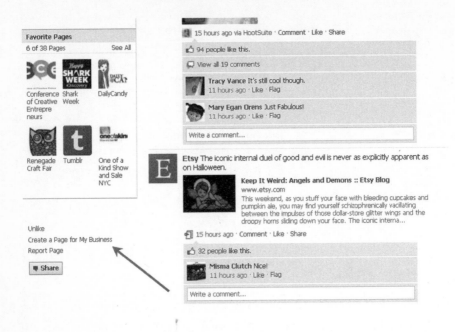

Now you are looking at the fan page setup. There are a few things here you need to make sure you get right! First is the category. There is an online store option under the "Brand, Product, or Organization" section. Make sure you pick this option. If you don't, you will be limited on the info you can put in the "About" section. Second is the name you want to call your online store. This will be the name of your fan page and cannot be changed, so double check what you are typing in. Also, make this the same as your Etsy shop, so you can start branding yourself across the board. Next, of course, is to verify you are authorized to run this page, and then you can enter your signature, which is your full name, first and last, that you signed up with when you created your Facebook page. Hit "Create" and you are ready to roll!

You are looking at your new fan/business page. Not very fancy—yet! Your picture/avatar is a small but very important part of your fan page. Your fans will start to associate your avatar with you. This is branding at its best.

Your avatar for your page will show up all over Facebook once you start linking and growing fans that link to your page. The

Create a Page

Community Page

Generate support for your favorite cause or topic by creating a Community Page. If it becomes very popular (attracting thousands of fans), it will be adopted and maintained by the Facebook community. Learn more.

Please note that you will not be able to edit the name of a Page after it has been created.

Page name:

(examples: Elect Jane Smith, Recycling)

[Create Community Page]

Official Page ←

Communicate with your customers and fans by creating and maintaining an official Facebook Page.

Please note that you will not be able to edit the name of a Page after it has been created.

Create a Page for a:

○ Local business

○ Brand, product, or organization

○ Artist, band, or public figure

Page name:

(examples: Summer Sky Cafe, Springfield Jazz Trio)

☐ I'm the official representative of this person, business, band or product and have permission to create this Page.
Review the Facebook Terms

[Create Official Page]

following figure shows where you can edit and add a new picture. Once you load your picture, you can move it around and save!

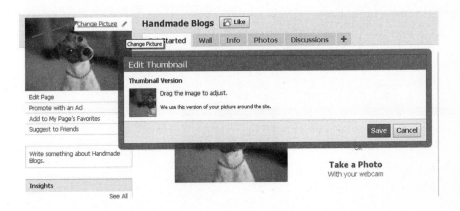

Here are some guidelines when you are making your picture/avatar:

Facebook specs recommend that profile pictures should be 200px wide, while height can vary as needed. What is less documented is how the thumbnail that Facebook uses across the system is generated from this picture. You'll find that the system crops images when generating a thumbnail, losing information around the edge. After some initial testing, I've determined that there's a "title safe" area within all images. So when you create your profile image that's 200px wide, allow a 12-pixel border around crucial information (such as typography or a logo) to allow for automatic cropping. Keep in mind that, whatever the shape of your profile image, Facebook thumbnails are square and sized based on the length of the shortest side of your image. So when designing rectangular profile pictures, make sure to keep your desired thumbnail imagery within a square boundary.

You can see my avatar at work in the following figure. I have my avatar set so that the words *Timothy Adam Designs* doesn't get cropped when Facebook crops the picture. Follow the preceding guidelines and your avatar will look perfect!

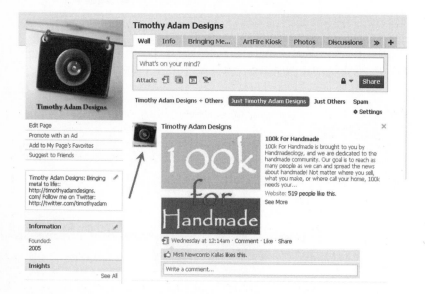

Now you can add all your detailed info. Here, you can include as many sites as you like. You may want to take your profile from your Etsy shop and fill in the company info, mission, and products. This will save you time and keep the branding trend going!

Promoting Your Products and Links on Facebook

A key strength of Facebook—especially for the new public profiles—is the viral spread of shared links into news feeds, using the

Links application. When anyone links to your site using this, the application presents the user with a number of images from the page that can be chosen as a thumbnail to accompany the link. This works perfectly when you are linking one of your Etsy items. You are given an option of pictures to pick from, and the text from your listing shows up. Make sure you pick a picture that shows off your product and is not blurry.

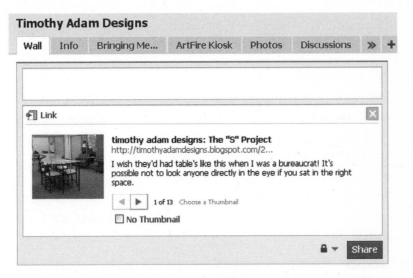

Adding Links from Your Blog or Another Blog

When linking a post, the text that is next to the picture most likely will not fit with the post you are linking to. The text is usually the description of the blog. This is fine, as long as you post some text above the picture so your friends know what the link is actually about. Make sure you pick the right picture. Adding pictures makes your links more viral—people are more likely to click on a link with a picture. Also, keep your text short. Try to stick to 150 characters; long text can turn friends or fans off. Short and simple is better (see following screen shot).

Facebook Insights

Your fan page comes equipped with some very powerful stats. Not only can you see the traffic to your fan page, you can see what

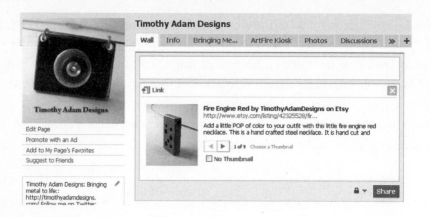

info is being viewed. Most importantly, you can see the demographic stats of the people that are visiting your fan page. This is the first time that we as Etsians can have access to this information. Your fan page is giving you a look into what gender and age groups are visiting your page, and eventually going to your shop.

In the following screen shot you can see where to find your insights. This option will not be available until you make your fan page public. You will also have to wait 48 hours until data starts to show up.

Once you have an audience and know who they are, you can start catering the info you provide on your fan page to who they are. For example, if you know your audience/fans are made up of more women than men, you most likely wouldn't want to post info about power tools. You get the idea.

You can also look at the different posts you make throughout a given week. See what brings you the most hits and interactions. If you notice that posting a link with a picture brings the most traffic, then stick with that method.

Also, when you are gathering more fans by promoting, you can see what techniques are working the best for getting more fans. For example, if you took out an ad for your fan page and you noticed that you got more fans in the time that your ad was running, you may want to run another ad like that.

Promoting Your Facebook Fan Page

The first step in promoting your Facebook fan page is to invite all your friends! You can select all your friends and send them an invitation to join your fan page. You have to click on them one by one. This may sound like a time-consuming task, but I did it with 1,600 friends. After inviting all my Facebook friends, in less than 24 hours I had 500 fans to my page.

Final Words

Facebook is an amazing viral means of promoting your online shop. Your fan page allows you to connect with your fans and your customers. When you are connecting and holding conversations with your fans, you are building your brand. If you promote your fan page and provide your fans a place to interact, your fan page will grow, and in turn, so will your sales.

10

Top Etsy Seller Interviews

I had the extreme privilege of asking eight top sellers on Etsy a series of questions. These sellers come from a diverse range of categories, such as soap making, photography, candle making, silk screening, vintage tags, knitting and crocheting, glass beads, and vintage clothing. You will find out how these sellers got their start in their craft and how they came to be a seller on Etsy. Each seller's interview also takes a look at their daily life as a top seller, and answers some of the questions we all want to know; for example, "What are a few things you have learned about shipping you could share with new Etsy sellers?" and "How do you not get lost in the crowd?" The answers to these questions and many more will help you as you start your journey as an Etsy seller.

Eight Top Etsy Sellers

Paula, Venbead

1,900 Sales in the Handmade Glass Bead Category

When and how did you become interested in making jewelry?

I've had a love affair with jewelry making since 1994 when, on my first wedding anniversary, I walked into a

(continued)

(continued)

Eight Top Etsy Sellers

little bead store in Boston's Haymarket Square and picked up a handmade bead. It started with polymer clay and moved into semiprecious gems and silver. The glass bug hit in early 2005 while I was reading a *Bead and Button* magazine article about a borosilicate bead artist, Emily Lake. I had never seen borosilicate glass before, but I felt drawn to it. After that, I started buying boro beads from self-representing artists to incorporate into my bracelets. Then it occurred to me that I could probably learn how to make them myself. In the spring of 2005, I took a

Eight Top Etsy Sellers

wonderful nine-week lampworking class at the Worcester Center for Crafts taught by the very talented Jennifer Geldard, and in July 2005, I set up a glass studio in my home. I have been happily melting glass ever since. Recently, I have added metalwork and enameling to my skill set in a never-ending desire to raise the bar for my work.

How did you find Etsy, and why did you start selling on Etsy?

I belong to a glass forum called lampworketc.com, and in 2007 some of the threads were about this really great site called Etsy for selling handmade. I was doing a lot of home parties and craft shows at the time, but I had a secret desire to find a wider customer base. I was also selling a little bit on eBay but was getting discouraged with the auction format. In May 2007, I sat down at my computer and really impulsively set up an Etsy shop. I listed six items that day, and I sat back and waited.

When I first started selling on Etsy, I was afraid of failing. Did you ever encounter that fear? If so, how did you overcome that fear?

I have to say I really wasn't afraid of failing because I was already selling my jewelry locally. I just didn't want to sacrifice the time away from my kids and husband to do it. The shows and parties were taking a toll on me, and I figured if this Etsy thing worked out, maybe I wouldn't have to do so many parties. I didn't really know what to expect from Etsy, and there wasn't anything else to compare it to. I knew I really liked the fact that it wasn't an auction-style site.

(continued)

(*continued*)

Eight Top Etsy Sellers

Do you remember your first sale on Etsy? How has your product changed since then?

I remember it was almost three months before my first item sold. I was so excited. The customer was from California, on the opposite coast from where I live in Rhode Island! I was amazed and I was hooked. When I look back at that pendant, I am proud because, while I feel I have become more skilled over the past three years, that pendant represented the very best I had to offer my customers at that time. It's still a well-made, pretty pendant, and the passion I feel for hot glass is very apparent in the piece.

Do you still get that "feeling" when you see your sold item number go up?

It's a total rush every time I make a sale. I never ever take it for granted. I feel so honored that in a sea of thousands and thousands of jewelry sellers, that buyer has chosen my work. They are choosing to spend their hard-earned dollar on something I made. That is very cool indeed.

What is one thing you love about Etsy and one thing you would like to see changed?

Oh, there is so much about Etsy I love. I think one of the best things about Etsy is that the typical Etsian is already hooked on handmade. They are a discriminating buyer, and they appreciate a well-made, beautiful piece of glass. I don't have to explain to them how my beads and pendants are different from the ones they might find at the craft store like I so often do at a craft show. They

Eight Top Etsy Sellers

already get it, and that is why they are in my shop. Etsy has enriched my life by bringing me such incredible customers. I love my Etsy shop. Changes are scary because Etsy is working for me. I hate to see changes because, often, what you ask for is not what you get, so I haven't asked Etsy for much. There are some technical tweaks I'd like to see to help me organize things. I'd love convos and sold items to be searchable. I'd also like a "sell similar" button.

Run through your typical day.

I work three days a week as a clinical social worker, so on those days my Etsy work is done early in the morning and at night. On my two days off a week, I spend an hour or two after the kids are off to school photographing what I have made the night before and listing new items. I then get my shipping ready and head off to the gym and the post office (if I have international packages). Then it's back home to shower and check my Etsy shop. I'll list a few more new items and or I'll relist something already in my shop, and I'm off to do errands and pick the kids up from school. While the kids are doing homework, I'm on Flickr and Facebook and, of course, relisting again. Then I make dinner, get the kids settled, and head down to my basement studio to torch for two or three hours. I pop upstairs to see the kids and put them to bed, and when I am done torching, I spend time watching TV with my husband while simultaneously checking my Etsy shop from my new iPad. It is also during these late hours that I get some of my most creative ideas, so I always have a sketchbook or pad handy. Then it's off to bed, and the whole cycle starts over. My life is about balance.

(continued)

(*continued*)

Eight Top Etsy Sellers

Product photography is so important when selling on Etsy. What are your tips for outstanding product photography?

I have learned a lot about taking pictures over the past three years. When I look back at some of my first pictures in my Etsy shop, I shudder. I think it's super-duper important to invest in the best possible camera you can afford with the best macro lens money can buy. Once you have this piece of equipment, then you need to do anything and everything to learn how to use it. My lampwork forum has a photography section, and I read every single thread I could on taking product photos. I bought tutorials, and I asked others to teach me. I traded my work with a photographer for an afternoon of lessons on how to adjust my camera settings and use my light booth properly. I also did a lot of web

Eight Top Etsy Sellers

surfing to investigate what made for eye-catching jewelry photos.

What are a few things you have learned about shipping you could share with new Etsy sellers?

For a long time I went to the post office for all my shipping. I got to know my postal people so well, I was bringing them cookies and bagels. Now it's my mail carrier I spoil. Somewhere after year one on Etsy I discovered PayPal shipping, bought a scale, and never looked back. I now ship everything domestic right from home. I *love* it. I only get to see my friends at the post office for the international packages, and while I miss their smiling faces, I don't miss the long lines and irritable customers.

Do you use social media like Facebook and Twitter to promote your Etsy shop? If so, what has been most effective for you?

I have a personal Facebook and one for my business. I have a Twitter account, and it's set up to tweet automatically when I list something (I know, I know—so spammy, so 2009). There's a lot of twitterlove on Etsy, but for me it's not visual enough. All those words floating by make me so anxious I feel like I'm at a cocktail party I wasn't invited to trying to make small talk with total strangers speaking in a foreign language. Where I have really found a comfortable place is on Flickr. I love the visual aspect. I love having an online gallery of my work, and I have gotten so many new customers from uploading my pics to Flickr groups.

What are your best tips for managing your time between Etsy and the rest of your life?

Get an iPad. No, seriously. Etsy is the rest of my life.

(continued)

(*continued*)

Eight Top Etsy Sellers

QUESTIONS FROM *HANDMADEOLOGY* FANS

How did you determine what your target customer base is?

They found me. I was doing something really original with the lampwork beaded key in 2007. I was the first Etsian to make a boro lampwork bead on the shaft of a skeleton key. The keys really took off, and I found my customer base. She's an edgy, hip, slightly-above-the-trend woman looking for something very original and fun. She's a sentimental girl who has an appreciation for old, worn, but well-loved objects that have been updated with the smooth, modern, sometimes futuristic-looking artisan glass and personalized just for her.

How do you know you are ready to start selling your items on Etsy?

You are ready to sell your items on Etsy when you are already selling them wherever you go. I think in order to be successful on Etsy, you need to be at a place where you don't need to ask that question. Your items rock out loud and you know that already—you just need a place to launch them out into the world. A home base.

What is the number one way to market your Etsy shop on the web to drive more traffic to sell your creations?

I don't think there is a universal number one. I think there's a number one for each person because not every social media outlet is right for everyone. I have already expressed my Twitter phobia, but for my friend Twitter is like food and air. I think she even tweets in her sleep. For me, Flickr has been my biggest view booster.

Eight Top Etsy Sellers

What tools do you use for your craft that you can't live without?

Well, that would be my torch and kiln because without those two items my craft would not be possible.

How do you not get lost in the crowd?

I am constantly striving to stand out. Once the beaded lampwork key caught on and every glassmaker out there was making them, I turned mine into necklaces by making charms with hand-stamped sayings. When I was copied again, I learned how to etch metal so I could add very unique things to my keys things that no one else would have. I also took many weekend classes with experts in my field to build my skill level to a place I am really proud of. I have recently added metalworking and enameling to my skill set in an effort to stay ahead of the pack, and I am constantly looking for new and original ways to showcase my glass. Be original. Make things that people want to copy, and when they do, move on, grow, change, evolve. Always evolve.

How much time will I need to dedicate to my shop to keep ahead of the pack?

A lot. I am just starting out as an official business and have just finished all my paperwork for taxes and preparing for taxes. . . .

Is there anything (program, web site, service, etc.) that you use to help minimize the time spent on the least favorite but most time-consuming part of running a business?

My filing system is atrocious, and I spend one day sometime in late January/early February scrambling to get my tax stuff together, so I am probably not the girl to ask.

(continued)

(continued)

Eight Top Etsy Sellers

Do you feel it is necessary to give away freebies with your product orders to encourage repeat customers?

Oh, yes. I love to pamper my customers. I like nice packaging. I love free gifts. I want them to feel as though they have just received a present from a good friend. The more my customers return, the better the gifts get. I keep a bowl of experimental and orphan beads and pendants for this purpose. I think the gifts and small surprises also encourage or remind people to leave feedback, which I love. Even if they don't leave formal Etsy feedback, I love getting e-mails or convos from my customers telling me how much they are enjoying my work. One customer had bought a glass heart and had me include a sterling paw print in memory of her beloved dog that had recently died. Through convos, I had learned the dog's name, and so I included a free and surprise hand-stamped tag with the dog's name. My customer had such a lovely, lovely response to this gift that she made me cry. That kind of experience is priceless.

How do you keep your shoppers from bouncing and get them to stay and buy?

I tell stories in my listings. I have a terribly neglected blog, so I use my listings to engage my customers, and I tell them things about my life or my kids through my jewelry.

Are you ever afraid your business will grow too much?

Sometimes I think I'm hindering growth because of that fear. LOL! No, I'm not afraid of that because

Eight Top Etsy Sellers

I always have the power to say no. I have been asked to consign and wholesale, and up until very recently I wasn't ready to take that step, so I would just politely decline. I feel pretty much in control of my own destiny. It's my passion and what makes my heart sing, and I am very humble about it all being a gift. I'm thoroughly enjoying each and every stage of my artistic growth and my business growth. Don't let it get away from you by doing anything that sucks the passion out of it.

Do you really make what you love, or do you create what you know (hope) will sell?

Oh, I make what I love and what I know others will love, too. If they don't love it as much as I do, perhaps I don't make it as much, maybe just for me and mom, and then I move on to find something else I love.

What was your turning point? What changed your sales from a little to a lot, if you weren't selling a lot right off?

My beaded skeleton keys. Once I started listing them, they took off, and when I strung them into necklaces and tagged them with steampunk, it was like a little rocket launch. I sold the first beaded key necklace I listed within two hours. I had tagged it with shabby chic, and a lampwork friend of mine who had been selling on Etsy for a lot longer than I sent me a convo telling me I was off my nut to be tagging such an obviously steampunk item incorrectly. I changed the tag, sold the key, and the rest is history.

Eight Top Etsy Sellers

Donna, Birdie Lane

13,000 Sales in the Vintage Category on Etsy

When and how did you become interested in making tags?

I became interested in making tags about three-and-a-half years ago. I wanted something special for a special gift, not a mass-marketed, barely worthy of notice gift tag, so I designed my own. It gave my gift that special and unique look that I was after, and the recipient loved it!

Eight Top Etsy Sellers

I was so pleased that it was a success—so much so that I began designing more tags.

How did you find Etsy, and why did you start selling on Etsy?

When I first saw Etsy, it looked very basic and not really professional. I had seen it mentioned on several different blogs and thought I'd check it out. I wasn't impressed, lol! I never gave it another thought for months. I had started making soldered pendants, and a few friends bought some and suggested that I sell them to the public at large. Living in a small town there weren't really any venues for doing that, so once again Etsy came to mind, though I didn't think that it would be the place to sell them at either. I was pleasantly surprised to see that Etsy had changed very much—and changed for the better. It was much more professional looking and had a ''WOW'' factor going for it. I made the decision that day to join up, though it took me about a week to find the courage to actually list anything!

When I first started selling on Etsy, I was afraid of failing. Did you ever encounter that fear? If so, how did you overcome that fear?

I was terribly afraid that no one would like my items and that failure surely awaited me. I was literally sweating with apprehension as I listed my first few items! I finished up and thought to myself that I didn't have much to lose and I just would *never* tell anyone that I had tried selling online. I thought I would just keep my silly foray of selling online my little secret. Much to my surprise, within about 20 minutes I had sold two pendants! I was hooked! That was all I needed to give me the confidence to continue!

(continued)

(continued)

Eight Top Etsy Sellers

Do you remember your first sale on Etsy? How has your product changed since then?

I referred to my first sale on Etsy in the question above. I branched out into making journals and such, but finally found that my niche was gift tags. Less time consuming than all the other items, and I could produce them in a very timely manner. I started out using an ink-jet printer, and my designs were simple. I now use a laser-jet printer and have come a long way in my design ability!

Do you still get that "feeling" when you see your sold item number go up?

I sure do! I always feel elation at the rising numbers. Knowing that my tags will adorn a special gift, be integrated in someone's artwork, used at their wedding, party, shower—just whatever—always makes me feel good.

What is one thing you love about Etsy and one thing you would like to see changed?

Etsy has brought me in contact with so many wonderful people, buyers and sellers alike. I have shipped my tags to nearly every country on the map and that in itself gives me a bit of a thrill!

I'm not too picky, and I really can't think of anything of any great magnitude that I would want changed about Etsy. It seems as though there was a standstill for a bit, but I do believe that Etsy is trying to forge ahead and introduce things that are helpful to both the sellers and buyers. Perhaps they realize now that it's the sellers that make Etsy the great venue that it is.

Run through your typical day.

A typical day for me begins around 7 AM and can last up to 2 AM in the morning. I start by checking orders and

Eight Top Etsy Sellers

I start printing. After getting each order printed, I start cutting, then it's on to putting it all together. There are holes to be punched, seam binding cut, tags to be strung and put into cello bags. Then they are topped with a bag topper (I no longer put a topper on every set of tags though, that helped cut down on some time spent doing that). The order is then wrapped as though it was a gift, packaged, and weighed. Shipping labels are printed, applied, and now comes the part my dog Charlie loves. I holler "ani-mail," and he's ready for the little jaunt to the mailbox!

(continued)

(continued)

Eight Top Etsy Sellers

Product photography is so important when selling on Etsy. What are your tips for outstanding product photography?

I'm lucky; I can scan most of my items! I find that it gives a more realistic representation of my product. I do have to photograph the seam binding that I sell, but with a good camera, the right lens, and proper lighting, it's not all that difficult to get a good picture, but oh so important! You want your items to be presented as attractively as possible. Blurry pix and dark lighting can certainly prevent a sale.

What are a few things you have learned about shipping you could share with new Etsy sellers?

Use PayPal to pay for and print your shipping labels! Also make use of the USPS "Shipping Assistant." You'll be doing yourself a big favor by eliminating countless time-consuming and costly trips to the post office! Be sure you package your items properly so they don't get damaged in shipping. Even that won't ensure that your package won't be mishandled by some overzealous postal worker, but at least you have the satisfaction of knowing you did what you could, and it will cut down on damage. Now if we could only come up with a surefire fix for lost packages!

Do you use social media like Facebook and Twitter to promote your Etsy shop? If so, what has been most effective for you?

I find that relisting is the best form of advertising for me. The Facebook thing and Twitter just isn't my thing!

What are your best tips for managing your time between Etsy and the rest of your life?

What???? You have a life???? Lol:)

Eight Top Etsy Sellers

Lauren, DearGoldenvintage

4,600 Sales in the Vintage Clothing Category on Etsy

When and how did you become interested in vintage clothing?

I grew up pretty poor, so the thrift store is where most of my clothing came from anyway, I suppose I was just drawn to the older clothing even then, and then when I was high school, it was impossible to buy the clothing the kids were wearing that came from the mall, so I started wearing vintage 1950s dresses all the time, which were way cheaper, and it just sort of stuck with me!

Do you remember your first sale on Etsy? How has your product changed since then?

Yep! A little pair of sandals, and since then I have refined the vintage in my shop and have a more 1930s–1950s focus.

(continued)

(*continued*)

Eight Top Etsy Sellers

Do you still get that "feeling" when you see your sold item number go up?

Completely and utterly.

What is one thing you love about Etsy and one thing you would like to see changed?

The checkout system is the biggest hassle. Nonpaying buyers result, and that's always frustrating.

Run through a typical day at Dear Golden.

Well, I get up at around 7:30 and start working and don't stop until around midnight, and that's totally normal. After nearly two years, I still have not figured out how to stop working. Daily, there is listing, garment cleaning, photo shooting, buying more vintage, packing and shipping, responding to customers—the tasks seems endless sometimes.

What are a few things you have learned about shipping you could share with new Etsy sellers?

Don't ship shoes to Italy!

Eight Top Etsy Sellers

What are your best tips for managing your time between Etsy and the rest of your life?

I wish I had some! I am terrible at this. I hope to "find my life" again someday!

Are you ever afraid your business will grow too much?

Sometimes I think I'm hindering growth because of that fear. Oh yes, and then I worry it'll crash; it's a constant push-pull of worry.

Eight Top Etsy Sellers

Dennis, dennisanderson

32,000 Sales in the Handmade Category on Etsy

(*continued*)

(*continued*)

Eight Top Etsy Sellers

When and how did you become interested in soap making?

It all started in a chemistry class I had in college, where in lab, we made some castile soap.

How did you find Etsy, and why did you start selling on Etsy?

Originally, I did not intend to sell my soap at all. My fiancée, Brandy, opened a shop selling jewelry and accessories in February 2007. I was at a dead-end job with one newborn and another on the way, so we decided that it would be good for extra income for me to start selling soap on Etsy.

When I first started selling on Etsy, I was afraid of failing. Did you ever encounter that fear? If so, how did you overcome that fear?

I never really had that fear at all. Whatever we sold was just some extra income from what I made at work.

Do you remember your first sale on Etsy? How has your product changed since then?

I do! I made a soap bar, took a picture, listed it on Etsy, and eight minutes later it sold! I haven't really changed my aesthetic too much. I bought a decent camera to get better pictures and went to a thrift store to pick up things for backgrounds of my shots.

Do you still get that "feeling" when you see your sold item number go up?

I still get it, believe it or not. Our goal after providing stellar service to our customers is to be the top handmade seller on Etsy.

Eight Top Etsy Sellers

What is one thing you love about Etsy and one thing you would like to see changed?

I love the fact that to me it's such an elementary listing process. It makes the not-so-computer-literate people able to list their creations. I think the only thing I would like seen changed is having our items sold or disappeared from the shop when payment has been made, and in between payment have them frozen so if they are OOAK (one of a kind) items, they won't sell twice.

Run through your typical day at the Anderson Soap Company.

I wake up in the morning, have a cup of coffee, and get my day started. Either Brandy or I will be making products to fill orders, or we will be shipping orders. We both rotate to make things run smoother. In between everything, since we work at home, we tend to our attention-seeking three- and four-year-old girls. Usually at about 2 to 3 PM, I get my mind off the business by playing games online, mainly Texas hold'em poker. I spend the rest of the day just getting things that need to be done online, or at my home.

(continued)

(*continued*)

Eight Top Etsy Sellers

Product photography is so important when selling on Etsy. What are your tips for outstanding product photography?

I would get a decent camera made for close-up shots and have it cleaned on a regular basis. Natural lighting, for me at least, is very important as well.

What are a few things you have learned about shipping you could share with new Etsy sellers?

I learned to do my shipping in batches anywhere between 10 and 35 orders a day. When I first started, I did them one at a time. I also streamlined my shipping, which means I have a designated area where the finished product is, and a table in front of it so I can just pull orders quickly. Also, I would like to add that international shipping is pricey.

Do you use social media like Facebook and Twitter to promote your Etsy shop? If so, what has been most effective for you?

I do have them, and I do use them. I don't like to use them too much, though, because it makes me feel like I am a spammer. I have to admit, I do use the Facebook more, only because I linked Facebook with Twitter, so any of my business Facebook posts automatically goes to Twitter.

What are your best tips for managing your time between Etsy and the rest of your life?

I don't think I can help you on this one. Etsy and my company are always on my mind, so there is no rest for the wicked.

Eight Top Etsy Sellers

Irene, Irenesuchocki

5,200 Sales in the Photography Category on Etsy

When and how did you become interested in photography?

I first became interested in photography in the mid-1990s. I started traveling and wanted to learn about photography so that I could take decent photographs on my trips. I took a night course at a college to learn how to use my camera. I became much more serious about photography in 2005 when I purchased my first digital SLR and found Flickr.

(continued)

(*continued*)

Eight Top Etsy Sellers

How did you find Etsy, and why did you start selling on Etsy?

I noticed that a couple of my Flickr contacts were selling prints on a site with a weird name: Etsy. I wasn't even thinking about selling prints at that time, but a seed must have been planted and the idea began slowly percolating in the back of my mind. About a year later, in early 2007, I opened a shop. Initially, it was simply a means to make a little extra money to pay for all the photography gear I was coveting.

When I first started selling on Etsy, I was afraid of failing. Did you ever encounter that fear? If so, how did you overcome that fear?

I wasn't afraid at the start. I didn't have many expectations at first, and I had a full-time day job. The start-up costs were minimal, the risk was low, and at that time there was no thought of doing it full time. I decided to quit my day job in May 2008. Then, in September, the economy crashed. Then, hello fear. The way I live with it is to have a Plan B and a Plan C. Last year, I started photographing weddings to diversify myself and to develop a new skill set. If sales ever seriously slump, I can seek more wedding and portrait work. My Plan C is to go back to what I was doing before (technical writing), at least on a part-time basis. So far, I have been blessed and feel so fortunate to be making a living doing what I love in this tough economy.

Do you remember your first sale on Etsy? How has your product changed since then?

Yes! I sold my first print the day after I opened my shop. It was so exciting! At first I only offered photographic prints. Over time, I have added other products

Eight Top Etsy Sellers

such as greeting cards, calendars, and photo jewelry (in collaboration with another Etsy seller). I also offer a matting service, and I work with a local professional framer to offer framed prints at a reasonable price. My style has evolved over time as well. My color palette has shifted from darker colors to lighter hues. I feel it has gotten more impressionistic and abstract over time, too.

Do you still get that "feeling" when you see your sold item number go up?

Oh, yes! I feel that little jolt in the heart region every time.

What is one thing you love about Etsy and one thing you would like to see changed?

I love that Etsy allows me to making a living doing what I love. It provides the infrastructure that supports the handmade and DIY ethos. I wasn't trained as an artist or a photographer, and I don't think I could have gone the route that artists traditionally have gone: the gallery system and agents. It doesn't suit my personality. I love dealing with people directly. I also love the support that sellers get through the Storque blog and forums. It's really quite phenomenal. I would like to see a better-functioning search. I realize that improvements are being made, but searching through the gazillions of items on Etsy is still a harrowing experience.

Run through your typical day.

- I usually wake up at around 7:30 and have a leisurely breakfast over the previous night's *Colbert Report.*

- I then log onto Etsy to check for sales and convos.

(continued)

(*continued*)

Eight Top Etsy Sellers

○ I respond to convos and e-mails and visit some of my favorite blogs to ease into the day.

○ I go for a walk or a jog mid-morning.

○ I like combining my shipping days with other errands to free up time on other days. On these days, I pick up prints at my lab in the morning; take prints that need framing to my framer; sometimes drop off prints at the gallery in Old Montreal, where some of my prints are sold; and then spend the afternoon packing up orders and going to the post office.

○ My creative days are spent sifting through my archive of photographs to identify those that I want to work on, processing photographs in Photoshop, experimenting with techniques in Photoshop, looking at books or web sites for inspiration, visualizing photographs that I want to take, and daydreaming about places I want to travel to. If the weather is nice or interesting, I'll get out for a couple of hours to shoot some new photographs. I love the flexibility that I have to do what I want when it's my creative time.

○ I blog a couple of times a week and try to update my Facebook status once a day, though I don't always succeed.

○ I'm trying harder these days to not work so much during the evenings, though if my boyfriend is out, I'll usually drift over to the computer. Otherwise, I'll do a bit of reading or, if my boyfriend is in, we'll catch up on our favorite shows.

Eight Top Etsy Sellers

Product photography is so important when selling on Etsy. What are your tips for outstanding product photography?

I'm lucky in that once I've created my final print-ready image, my product shot is also ready. But the following tips can help to improve any product shot:

○ Make sure the images are sharp.

○ Use simple backgrounds.

○ Use soft lighting to avoid harsh shadows. You can shoot outdoors on an overcast day or in shade, use window light, or a light box. Avoid using direct on-camera flash, which creates harsh lighting.

(continued)

(*continued*)

Eight Top Etsy Sellers

○ Edit your image file in a program like Photoshop or Photoshop Elements. A simple levels adjustment to increase the dynamic range (from the shadows to the highlights) will dramatically improve your photographs.

Do you use social media like Facebook and Twitter to promote your Etsy shop? If so, what has been most effective for you?

I just recently started using Facebook. I resisted for a long time, fearing the time-suckage factor. I can't tell yet how effective it has been for me, but my entire online selling philosophy has been to just keep putting myself out there without regard for immediate results. I like to think of every online communication as a little ripple that gets sent out into the online universe. Some of those ripples may end up carrying someone back to me, be it a stock agency that wants to license my images, a potential wedding client, or someone who responds to and connects with my work and ends up ordering a print. You never know who is going to find you where, so the more places you can be found, the better. Twitter is next!

What are your best tips for managing your time between Etsy and the rest of your life?

I'm probably not the best person to ask. I don't have children, and now that I work from home, the line between work and life is very blurry indeed. I have to be very disciplined in this regard and create rules for myself like "Do not, repeat, do not check the computer after 10:00 PM." Let's just say I'm working on it.

Eight Top Etsy Sellers
Amber, knottybabywear

17,000 Sales in the Crochet and Knitting Category on Etsy

When and how did you become interested in crocheting?

Just weeks after having my first child, I found myself home all alone for days on end (my husband drives a truck)

(*continued*)

(continued)

Eight Top Etsy Sellers

with this tiny person who could not really talk to me and would barely stay awake for more than an hour at a time. So I bought the book *I Can't Believe I'm Crocheting* and some yarn and taught myself to crochet. That was back in 2003.

How did you find Etsy, and why did you start selling on Etsy?

I found Etsy in 2006 by accident. I was blog surfing and came upon a blog who was raving about The Black Apple that had links to her Etsy shop. From there, I fell in love. I was already selling my handmade baby hats, sweaters, blankets, and other things in a local collective boutique called Made in Chico, but they were taking 30 percent of my sales. So when I stumbled onto Etsy, it was love at first sight!

When I first started selling on Etsy, I was afraid of failing. Did you ever encounter that fear? If so, how did you overcome that fear?

Not really. This whole thing started out as a hobby but, over time, has developed into a full-time job. Everything I have done has been trial and error.

Do you remember your first sale on Etsy? How has your product changed since then?

Yes! My first sale was to my friend. I think she felt like she had to buy from me to show me she believed in me! My second sale was the one I count, though. It was a wholesale order of dresses. I had no idea what I was doing and sold them way too cheap just to make a sale. I got way too excited. My products have changed drastically over

Eight Top Etsy Sellers

the years. I target my products to two specific types of buyers: photographers and new moms. When I first started out, I didn't know who would buy my things or even if anyone would. I just made things I liked. These days, I am confident in my products, and I make things that I know other people want or need.

Do you still get that "feeling" when you see your sold item number go up?

Every day! Watching that number go up just proves to me that I am good at what I do and people like what I have to offer.

What is one thing you love about Etsy and one thing you would like to see changed?

I love what Etsy stands for. A place for artists and crafters to show and sell the items they make. The number one thing that needs to change is the customer service between Etsy and their sellers. After that, I would only complain about the shopping cart. It leaves much to be desired.

Run through your typical day.

I wake up at 6 AM, shower, dress, and then wake my kids. I drive my son (age 7) to school, which is 25 miles away, and then head straight back home. I then work non-stop on orders and answering convos until it is time to drive the 25 miles again to pick him up. Once we get home, its homework time, dinnertime, bath time, bedtime. That is when I go back to work again making and filling orders, printing shipping labels and answering more convos through Etsy. Usually, I am in bed by midnight. Then it starts all over again.

(continued)

(continued)

Eight Top Etsy Sellers

Product photography is so important when selling on Etsy. What are your tips for outstanding product photography?

Buy a good camera! I use a Nikon D60 for the photos I take myself. I also have a handful of photographers who do product shots for me when I need them. Every one of those photographers are work-at-home moms just like me.

What are a few things you have learned about shipping you could share with new Etsy sellers?

Keep your shipping costs as low as possible. For the most part, the customer does not care about the extra frills if you deliver a quality product. And don't leave out Canada! Twenty-five percent of my business is Canadian, and shipping to Canada is oftentimes *less* than shipping within the United States.

Eight Top Etsy Sellers

Do you use social media like Facebook and Twitter to promote your Etsy shop? If so, what has been most effective for you?

Facebook has boosted my sales tremendously!! Having a fan page where my customers can get updates and sneak peaks, view photos, and have discussions with each other has allowed me to communicate with my customers on a more personal level. We are like a big family there on the fan page and are at 3,650 of us and growing daily!

What are your best tips for managing your time between Etsy and the rest of your life?

This is tough because I still haven't found balance. A lot of things have suffered at home because of the time I spend working. But I am slowly learning to take more breaks. I used to be afraid to put my shop into vacation mode, but I am doing it more this year, and I am realizing that my customers will wait for me. Because they are mostly all women and mothers, they understand when I need a few days to rest or catch up. So my time management is a work in progress.

QUESTIONS FROM *HANDMADEOLOGY* FANS

What tools do you use for your craft that you can't live without?

My sewing machine, my serger, my crochet hooks, and my favorite pair of scissors.

How do you not get lost in the crowd?

Stay relevant. Constantly expand and create new items to offer.

(*continued*)

(continued)

Eight Top Etsy Sellers

Do you feel it is necessary to give away freebies with your product orders to encourage repeat customers?

No. Please do not give away your hard work for free!

Do you really make what you love, or do you create what you know (hope) will sell?

Both! Most of my items are inspired by my customers, especially my crocheted hats. Nearly every single one was a suggestion by a customer, and I just made it come to life!

Eight Top Etsy Sellers

Suzanne, Bliss Soy Candles

1,500 Sales in the Candle-Making Category on Etsy

Eight Top Etsy Sellers

When and how did you start crafting, creating, making?

It was all by accident. In 2004, I read an article about melting candles together to make new ones. The thought of making candles popped into my head, and that's all it took. I already knew at the time that soy had numerous benefits including being clean-burning (with no to little soot) and burning longer. So I started doing research on the Internet and started buying materials to make my own candles.

As with anything else, halfway wasn't enough, and I had too many candles! I started to give them away to friends, who told me I should be selling them. So I made more to sell locally and realized I had too many. I signed up for what I thought would be a one-time craft show— Garfield Park in Grand Rapids, Michigan. It was then that I first heard the raving about my products—it was one of those things in life that takes you by surprise. I was addicted to the praise and signed up for several more shows. Within a year, I was honored by being invited to an invite-only show called Beneath the Wreath, and got into another show in Lowell that is next to impossible to get into. By 2008, I believe I was signed up for 20 shows!

How did you find Etsy, and why did you start selling on Etsy?

Another artist referred me to Etsy back in 2007. I wanted to expand my business and decided to give it a try.

When I first started selling on Etsy, I was afraid of failing. Did you ever encounter that fear? If so, how did you overcome that fear?

I often think about what I would need to do to just sell candles full time. That is where my fears come into play.

(continued)

(*continued*)

Eight Top Etsy Sellers

The uncertainty is very scary. After all, there is a mortgage payment and car payment to make! I have not overcome the fear yet, but I do continue to look at the numbers to try to determine if there is any possibility.

Do you remember your first sale on Etsy? How has your product changed since then?

I don't remember my first sale, but then my memory isn't what it used to be! My product has changed slightly. From the beginning, I had the decorative lids and same concept. All of my jar/lid combinations were my own "creation," and way back when I started, I didn't see anyone else with anything similar. Of course, the Internet sales sites weren't around either, or if they were, they weren't well known. The jars are a little larger now, and I have greatly improved my labels—both of which were great decisions. Appearance is important, which is part of why product photo quality is so critical. And who wouldn't want more wonderful soy wax in their jar? In recent years, I have also gotten more into gift packaging and what I can do to make things fun for gift recipients. I have done the Holiday Packs since about 2005, but the fun gift boxes and special touches are more recent.

Do you still get that "feeling" when you see your sold item number go up?

Absolutely! I love my customers, and I still get super excited when people order certain fragrances. Fall and food fragrances are my absolute favorites. It's kind of funny because you set a goal for yourself (like 1,000 sales), and then when you hit it, you have to make another goal so you get that excitement again. It's addictive!

Eight Top Etsy Sellers

What is one thing you love about Etsy and one thing you would like to see changed?

Etsy is like a family. Sure, you have your people out there who copy your items or are just not cordial, but for the most part everyone helps each other out. Etsy also has the best traffic of all of the selling sites in my personal experience. We have been asking for a shipping calculator forever. That would be my number one wish, with coupon codes being a close second wish list item. For me, it is very difficult not having those available.

Run through a typical day.

I still have my full-time job, so juggling is what I do. I fit in Etsy in every "free" moment that I have. I make candles and package in the evening and on the weekends, create UPS labels in the mornings, put the packages out at lunchtime, list here and there, jump on Facebook when I have a free moment—it's a good thing I have that touch of ADHD to keep me going!

(continued)

(continued)

Eight Top Etsy Sellers

Product photography is so important when selling on Etsy, what are your tips for outstanding product photography?

While I still have some photos that I know need work, this is one area that I have greatly improved. My biggest tips are to take advantage of natural light—it makes beautiful photos. A white background really makes items stand out. I love, love, love photos taken at unusual angles or outdoors in a natural setting. When I first started out, I had another Etsian suggest that I put "props" in my photos—sprigs of lavender, cinnamon, etc. Listen to suggestions. I'm so glad I did! One of the best items I ever got for free is my Nikon D40 camera. It takes wonderful photos. If you can get your hands on one of these, the camera alone will make a big difference. When you look at your photos, try to imagine what others will think. Ask yourself if it would make you look at the item. Sometimes an unusual photo is just the ticket to make your item stand out from the pack!

What are a few things you have learned about shipping you could share with new Etsy sellers?

As a beginner, you can't help but have a learning curve until you get a system. Simply put, there are some things you will learn as you go. If you do nothing else, invest in packaging! If you have fragile items, stock up on bubble wrap, paper, peanuts, good-quality boxes (thick boxes—not the USPS freebies), etc. Do not skimp or you will have breakage—it's inevitable. Even with my overkill on packaging, I will get a damage report on occasion. I am often reminded of the scene in *Ace Ventura* where he is posing as a delivery driver. I try to make sure "that" guy can't break my products. I just did a blog article on

Eight Top Etsy Sellers

shipping, encouraging people to try UPS. Ninety-nine percent of my shipping is done with them now. Their damage rate is much lower, and insurance is included. In addition, their tracking is "real time," and their rates are either lower or comparable in my case. They also offer a new Smart Pickup option, where you pay $10 a week and they pick up whenever you ship, even if it is all five days. For me, it is still less to ship with them than USPS, and again, there is insurance included! I never have to tell a customer they should have asked for insurance—it's a beautiful thing.

Do you use social media like Facebook and Twitter to promote your Etsy shop? If so, what has been most effective for you?

I have to admit, my Twitter is pretty much on "autopilot." I have most items automatically going to it via Twitterfeed. I do retweets and jump in when I can, but I find my time is more wisely spent on Facebook and blogging when time permits. I love the application RSS Graffiti on Facebook. It posts your Etsy, Artfire, Zibbet, and other listings per the schedule you set up. This means no more manually posting your listings to Facebook. This has definitely made a difference in my sales. On Facebook, you have to be sociable, let people know what you are up to, do product updates, etc. I also highly suggest having your blog posts go to your page automatically. That way, your fans are getting all the news they can in one place. While I haven't seen any sales from it, I suggest at least trying the Payvment application as well. They just added the ability to import your Etsy listings, so they are available to purchase right on your fan page. My goal is to get whatever

(continued)

(continued)

Eight Top Etsy Sellers

I can in that one place. I do the same with my blog. I just added some scheduled blogging days, too, and I am excited to see what those bring!

What are your best tips for managing your time between Etsy and the rest of your life?

You have to give yourself breaks somewhere. It really comes down to planning. I'm usually wiped out after packaging at night so I do my UPS labels in the morning while I'm getting ready for my real job. I squeeze in whatever I can throughout the day so that I can have a little "me" time in the evening. It doesn't happen every day, but it does happen. On weekends, I get the bulk of my work done right away so that I can move on to other things. Candle making is easier for me on weekends, so that is when I do the bulk of it. You have to figure out what works for you. If you have family, let them help you! You can get some quality time and you get to the things you really want to do faster.

As someone who used to work as a manager in manufacturing, I learned many things that help me in my business. I am very big on time efficiency. Save up those similar tasks so that you can do them all at the same time. For instance, waiting a couple of days to process orders may allow you to do "like" items all at once, and it saves you extra setups. This saved me last year when I was the Featured Seller. I printed my order reports by fragrance and processed orders that way. It was a lifesaver! Look at your setups. Is there something that could be done differently? Can the process be changed to be more efficient? Can you save a ton of time just by moving things around in your work area?

Eight Top Etsy Sellers

QUESTIONS FROM *HANDMADEOLOGY* FANS

How did you determine what your target customer base is?

From my very first day, I wanted to target customers who wanted a higher-end soy candle that had a special decorative appeal. As time went on, I found that customers purchased my candles for two reasons—quality and appearance. To this day, my target customers remain the same.

How do you know you are ready to start selling your items on Etsy?

When you get more people raving about them than just friends and family. You also need to make sure you have the time to commit and if you are not computer/tech savvy yourself, find someone who is. I still feel blogging, Facebook, photography, verbiage, and knowing when to list are necessities.

What is the number one way the market their Etsy shop on the web to drive more traffic to sell your creations?

Blogging and Facebook have been major drivers for me. Again, the RSS Graffiti app has definitely brought me more sales. As far as blogging goes, people love selling advice and product/artist features. I shouldn't forget the simple things either—business cards, thank you notes, coupons, and small samples in packages are huge. Add a referral discount program—people will refer more with an incentive! I have found mailings via snail mail do not work anymore for me. When you

(continued)

(continued)

Eight Top Etsy Sellers

consider this option, look at the sales generated versus the cost to mail. Even e-mail promotions, with permission, of course, don't have a major impact on my traffic unless I offer a huge sale, which I just can't do because while my pricing is higher, there is no "wiggle" room. My materials have a higher cost, so I'm a bit stuck in that regard. However, others may find e-mailed sales to be a great way to get some attention in their shop!

How do you not get lost in the crowd?

Do at least one listing in the morning, afternoon, and evening. Your goal should be to get people from all areas of the country into your shop. Remember, some people can be as many as three hours ahead of or behind you! Brag about your product on your blog and Facebook. How is your product different? Let people know. Keep your items and your shop fresh. Create new items. Rearrange your featured items.

Do you feel it is necessary to give away freebies with your product orders to encourage repeat customers?

The only thing I give is a single tea light sample. And while I did not believe in it at first, it has generated more sales and interest. I recommend giving one small thing away within reason that is affordable for you.

How do you come up with blog topics that you think will be interesting enough for others to read?

You can usually tell what is popular just by visiting the Etsy Forum. And, of course, people love to see themselves and others featured!

Eight Top Etsy Sellers

Do you really make what you love, or do you create what you know (hope) will sell?

For me, it is both. I love my candles. It is so awesome to get all of the wonderful comments from my customers and fans! I typically have a pretty good idea of what will sell. Sometimes new fragrances don't sell like I had hoped, but I am working on a plan to market the newbies better.

What was your turning point? What changed your sales from a little to a lot, if you weren't selling a lot right off?

I'm not really sure what the turning point was before being the Featured Seller in November 2009. That has definitely been the biggest change for me. Not only were there numerous sales from the Feature, but many of those customers have returned over and over for more candles. While the quality of my candles is critical to maintain to get repeat sales and referrals, I think some of the things I do have made the difference. Always thank your customers at least once—twice if you have the opportunity. I always make sure everything looks professional right down to the boxes the items are shipped in and the items enclosed (i.e., thank you cards, samples, etc.). People on Etsy purchase there because of the quality and personal touch. That big department store isn't going to hand-write thank you cards and send free goodies.

Eight Top Etsy Sellers
Bethany, Toy Breaker

12,000 Sales in the Men's Category on Etsy

When and how did you become interested in ties (love them BTW)?

The TieLab division came about very organically. One afternoon, I was playing around with making a printed jacket for my fiancé. I had a silkscreen prepared with a huge graphic already sized for a larger garment. In fears of ruining the jacket, I practiced first on a few vintage, World War II–issue, wool ties lying about the studio. (I'm a rabid comber of local antique and junk shops for photo and styling props.) I liked how they came out, edges truncated—I quickly photographed them and put them on Flickr.com, where I frequently archive and test market much of my

Eight Top Etsy Sellers

work. The next day, a few blogs picked up the images, and then a few more—and all of a sudden I had people e-mailing me out of nowhere demanding to get one (or many more). Thankfully, I'm adept at hand coding, and I put up a quick site for them by later that night.

People always ask me why I "just make ties," like it is a bad word. Ties are always spoken of with such derision and sneer. They're the perpetual punchline in songs, jokes, and consistently maligned as the most boring gift to give or receive. Think of Dad muttering, "Oh, a tie. Thanks." I wanted to change that. The necktie is such an interesting design problem; its shape gives the designer a challenging "canvas" to design on (dimension-wise, as it is so long and thin, unlike a T-shirt).

Conceptually, the tie is a traditionally hated object, one that symbolizes restraint, conformity, and is the symbol of corporate American drudgery. What fun and challenge is there in designing something that people already love? I enjoy subverting traditional tie patterns and motifs without venturing into gauche "novelty tie" territory. I have many clients who have jobs in the arts and want to wear something that is still artful, handmade, and well designed—but not stifling creatively.

From a business and online sales standpoint, choosing to design neckties makes sense, as the rate of return and exchange is minuscule with an accessory of an understood and established size. People know what they're getting size-wise with a necktie; therefore, I have far less inventory overhead than a shirt designer, who not only has to stock XS–XXL, but must make screens in quadruplicate to grade for the size difference.

(continued)

(continued)

Eight Top Etsy Sellers

How did you find Etsy, and why did you start selling on Etsy?

While working at Cranbrook Academy of Art, an architect friend of mine mentioned that I should try selling on Etsy, since people were starting to use it as a go-to venue for handmade work. (This was way back when dinosaurs roamed in early 2006!) Since I had already been running a successful stand-alone online shop of my own, it seemed like a logical extension of my existing web presence.

When I first started selling on Etsy, I was afraid of failing. Did you ever encounter that fear? If so, how did you overcome that fear?

Since I was already successfully operating my own online store and wholesaling to physical shops, I wasn't too afraid of failing there—it seemed mostly like a fun and low-risk chance to take for more exposure. I had initially looked at it as a way to bolster my existing avenues, but it quickly took over my life!

Do you remember your first sale on Etsy? How has your product changed since then?

My shop sat idle for quite a long time before I knew the ropes, but once I started spending more time on there and made my work visible, it took off quite quickly. My first sale was in the holiday season of 2006; had I a clue about not making 20 pieces available of each item, and instead relisting after sales, I would have done much better. My product has remained quite consistent to when I began selling on Etsy. As someone who is distracted easily, I have to discipline myself by focusing on one thing and doing that one thing to the very best of my abilities. As far as differences, hopefully my photos are far less rubbish! Even though I was both an

Eight Top Etsy Sellers

experienced photographer and online seller, looking back to some of my older presentations is a bit painful. With the growth of my business, I've been able to greatly increase the color, width, and fabric offerings—as well as transitioning from mainly single-tie sales to a large number of grouped packages suitable for wedding and commitment ceremonies.

Do you still get that "feeling" when you see your sold item number go up?

Of course! If that ever becomes just a chore, you should be doing something else.

What is one thing you love about Etsy and one thing you would like to see changed?

I love that there is a centralized place to purchase work directly from artists, and that I can feel confident spending my duckets with others who are committed to responsible manufacturing practices instead of a gross, big-box store.

From a selling standpoint, it's very difficult for printers and those who make multiples to function efficiently with the listing and cart system as is. A "select color" or "select size" button at checkout would save me hours and hours of work every day in answering questions about what is left, even though all the options are available. Even though I state that all colors shown are available in a listing, potential clients (myself included!) can have very short attention spans while shopping online and do not want to read a *War and Peace*–length item description. I've tried to circumvent this by listing more items in single colors, but now I'm finding people are hesitant to wade through a shop with over 300 items.

(*continued*)

(*continued*)

Eight Top Etsy Sellers

Run through a typical day.

Oh, boy. I do this full time. I'm up by 9 or 10—I hate mornings. Ten seconds down the stairs, open laptop, immediately start reading convos/e-mails. Start relisting items that sold overnight. Make espresso and feed the cats. Log in all the orders that came in overnight so I know what to print for the start of the day. This can take anywhere from an hour to eight, depending on volume and time of year. After all questions are answered and orders are checked in, drink more espresso and zoom down to the studio and start printing.

My home and studio are 15 minutes apart. I used to spout on about how it was "good to have psychological space from your work," but that's a big lie. I've found a way around it by having everything else but the printing and shipping part with me at all times on my laptop and iPhone. I'm a workaholic, and being away from what I'm making sends me into panic.

Most of the rest of the day is devoted to printing—to date, I've probably printed close to 35,000 ties myself, which is pretty physically demanding, but thankfully, as a result, I don't have to go to the gym! I'm a bit of a fanatic about staying in shape. I'm glad to have a profession that allows me to not just sit at a desk.

I try to remember to stop printing briefly before 3 PM if I need to take any photos of new designs or document custom colorways I've made so far that day. I use only natural light, and in the summer, the light is too yellow in the late afternoon; in the winter, well . . . not there at all.

Immediately after photo time, back to printing. I do check my e-mail every 15 to 20 minutes while printing to

Eight Top Etsy Sellers

see if anything new has come in. As most items are made to order, I try to keep as current as possible with what is in the queue so I can batch as many of the same prints together as possible to save time. By this time, I have quite a few items finished and ready to hand over to my best friend, who is my shipping assistant. He comes in later in the day and does the most important part, which is getting everything out the door to its destination. It doesn't matter how well you've made something if it doesn't arrive promptly or isn't presented well. He also brings me coffee and Boston creme donuts.

Sometimes I'll be at the studio printing till 10 PM, sometimes 4 AM or later. To me, anything less than a 12-hour workday is unacceptable. When I do go home, I try and wind down by editing photos, reading and answering more e-mails and convos, updating listings, and updating my main site, cyberoptix.com. Also some requisite tweeting, Facebooking, and Internet tomfoolery and posting requests for images from the press and blogs.

I try to shut my brain off and hit the hay sometime between 3 AM and 6 AM. (I've been known to relist and answer convos if I get up to pee in the middle of the night.) Yep, I have a problem!

This is mostly a production schedule, where I am right now in the year. At slower times, instead of so much printing and e-mail answering, the day is filled with design tweaks in Photoshop, scanning bits of vintage ephemera to be recombined into patterns, and testing color colorways that might appear great in one's head, but not so great in real life. Photo shoots with models, both in-studio and on location, are a welcome break from production printing.

(continued)

(*continued*)

Eight Top Etsy Sellers

Sometimes it's really sad and frustrating to hear rumors that people think that I'm outsourcing my work, but the fact is that my work is my life. I'm too much of a control freak to have it any other way. This is what I do, nonstop, and it's why I am able to produce a pretty high volume and still print it all myself. This schedule isn't for everyone. Thankfully, my other half is very understanding, though he does get a little lonely due to my long hours—we try to meet for dinner sometimes, which is nice. I have to run with it at this pace as long as I can. I'm very fortunate and thankful to have seen some success pretty early in life, and I can't shirk it just because there may be some other things I want to do during the day.

Product photography is so important when selling on Etsy. What are your tips for outstanding product photography?

Eight Top Etsy Sellers

From a buyer's perspective, one really wants to be able to clearly envision what he or she is getting, so the seller must balance being artful in presentation while being very true to the product.

I try to take some close-ups so the texture can be easily viewed, a long shot (not the first image, as this view is pretty boring visually) buyers really want to see where the print falls in relation to the entire object; the reverse side if it is important to the particular item, and a view of the product being worn on a model. I try to include an image of the tie on a body in as many item listings as possible. I'm pretty attached to those images, as they're usually my friends (and they're always quite handsome!) Unfortunately, I find that the model view doesn't work as well for selling ties when presented as the main image. If you have well-styled photos, people often don't think that you're selling a product in the photo—rather, the photo itself as an art piece—and this can be confusing in a treasury. I'm sure this is less of an issue for other, larger articles of clothing, but accessories can get lost in the whole composition of an outfit or styled location shoot. People need to immediately know what you're selling.

What are a few things you have learned about shipping you could share with new Etsy sellers?

Have options and don't be afraid of shipping internationally! If you make products that are under four pounds in weight, offer First Class International shipping instead of just Priority or Express, which can be very costly. International shipping never used to be fun, but something we've done anyway since the very beginning. I've been using Endecia (an electronic shipping service) for nearly a year,

(continued)

(*continued*)

Eight Top Etsy Sellers

and it is one of the best shipping changes/business decisions I've ever made. Their nominal monthly fee is worth it times 1,000 for the time and money saved waiting in line at the post office, especially for international packages. Endecia is one of the few ways you can send First Class International parcels without having to visit a postal human. With the continual downsizing of postal services across the United States, many are cutting their office hours, making it nearly impossible for busy folks to use counter-only services. I've also found that being able to fill out customs forms electronically (rather than using the old-fashioned, handwritten ones) speeds up delivery through border crossings. Not sure why, but my rate of loss has also really gone down significantly since using an electronic shipping service. The USPS "Click-n-Ship" free version helps, but at this time doesn't cover all international services like Endecia does.

Do you use social media like Facebook and Twitter to promote your Etsy shop? If so, what has been most effective for you?

I definitely do, but I'm also a serious Internet addict who has been online since 1992, so I see it as more fun than just a necessary marketing evil. Twitter to me is like being at a crowded bar. Be conversational—don't bombard people with endless item listings and treasury mentions; that gets really tiresome. The same is true for Facebook. If you have a story, tell it in small increments; people will be much more likely to be engaged that way.

I'm an unapologetic nerd, and the Internet (social media or otherwise) is my main way of communicating, not just in business. It's hard to say which has been the most effective

Eight Top Etsy Sellers

tool, since I use both of them pretty heavily and equally; they're both very different, and in three years, something completely different will probably be more important than either of them. Remember MySpace, Friendster, LiveJournal, your own blog? Didn't think so! Don't rely on any tool that is in favor at the present moment as the meat of your marketing strategy, I personally believe one should have a whole suite of ways to tickle the interest of potential customers.

What are your best tips for managing your time between Etsy and the rest of your life?

I don't have a "rest of your life," so I'm not the one to ask! I can't remember the last time I had a few hours off, never mind a day off. I'm hoping to achieve somewhat of a better balance this year—I'm going to start yoga again soon in hopes of attaining a little mind quieting, and more cooking and acquiring less of a take-out box collection.

QUESTIONS FROM *HANDMADEOLOGY* FANS

How did you determine what your target customer base is?

It's hard to say—mostly just in feedback from clients. They often tell me "I'm getting this to wear at X, Y, or Z event," and then I can infer a pretty accurate picture about who is shopping. I started making things for my friends; I obviously knew what their demographic was, and I like to think I have a few subsets—it is pretty well split between guys buying pieces for themselves and a strong gifting market. Guys mostly shop with me out of frustration with the regular department store fare.

(continued)

(*continued*)

Eight Top Etsy Sellers

What tools do you use for your craft that you can't live without?

My laptop. I do enjoy travel above all else, even if it's going to New York City for 24 hours for an event—if I have my sites, photos, and orders mobile, I can occasionally leave the studio for a day, and that is required to maintain sanity. Everything else is really low tech—no presses or even clamps, everything is positioned by hand and eye to 1/16 inch tolerances on a grid of registration marks. This allows for easy custom placements on request for clients, say if someone is atypically short or tall. It's pretty much just me and a squeegee, a mountain of screens, and some ink.

How much time will I need to dedicate to my shop to keep ahead of the pack?

I literally devote my whole day. I don't know any other way. If there's work to be done, my conscience just can't let me relax and go on to something else for the sake of enjoyment alone.

Do you feel it is necessary to give away freebies with your product orders to encourage repeat customers?

I find the freebie thing to not be viable, long haul, and honestly a little distasteful. I don't believe in promoting excess waste. Including a package full of tchochkes that may go unused is environmentally irresponsible and, to me, works to cheapen one's product. Also, what on earth does a Tootsie Roll have to do with a tie, and I sure don't want something like that melting in transit and ruining what someone took the effort to order. (I guess I'm still bitter over something I ordered from an Etsy seller that arrived covered in melted "free gifts.") I strongly believe it is better to keep one's prices fair at all times and not fall

Eight Top Etsy Sellers

into a trap of endless sales and free gifts as a way to entice people. I think it is far more important to channel that time and energy into sourcing better materials in order to keep prices low and fair consistently. Silk ties are $40; synthetic, $30. Simple. Customers know what they are getting into. I don't want to present my shop like a no parking sign in Boston: 20 percent off every third Thursday, but only in the two months leading up to a legal holiday, excluding November and December, only on pink and green items, and if you buy three, you get something you'll probably throw in a junk drawer. No thanks! Good customer service, engaging products, and a fair pricing structure should trump all else.

Do you really make what you love, or do you create what you know (hope) will sell?

I could never live with myself if I didn't make what I love. About the only concession I've made is with color—if I had my way, everything would be black on black. I do have a bit of a darker sensibility, but I realize that would be far too limiting. I recently caved in to offering both orange and yellow ties. I *hate* orange and yellow, but I can't force my chromophobia on everyone—that's not so nice!

Conclusion

This book is designed to provide a foundation for selling your hand-made goods online. I hope now that you have finished reading, you feel you have acquired the basic skills necessary get started selling on Etsy. The business of selling arts and crafts online is ever-changing. Learning and relearning is an ongoing process, as you have seen. To keep up to date with the most recent changes, news, and tips, visit Handmadeology.com.

About the Author

Timothy Adam is a self-taught metal artist and a certified Mig welder. He started designing modern metal furniture in 2004. He built his first piece in Baltimore with his sister-in-law, who is a furniture designer. He found his passion in metal and kept on designing and building. He struggled for three years to make a name in local galleries in the Grand Rapids, Michigan, area before a friend introduced him to Etsy in February 2007, and it completely changed his business. He started creating a jewelry line and has not turned back since. In November 2007, he had to quit his full-time day job because his passion of creating metal was becoming a dream come true! He is now selling all over the world through his Etsy shop. He also has wholesale accounts around the country with galleries, museums and salons.

Index

217